What Is Midrash?

What
Is
Midrash?

by
Jacob Neusner

Fortress Press
Philadelphia

Library of Congress Cataloging-in-Publication Data

Neusner, Jacob, 1932–
What is Midrash?
(Guides to biblical scholarship)
Bibliography: p.
1. Midrash — History and criticism. I. Title.
II. Series.
BM514.N49 1987   296.1'406   86–46423
ISBN 0-8006-0472-5

2547E87   Printed in the United States of America   1–472

For
DAVID and SONIA WEINER
on the occasion of their marriage

8 Tammuz 5746
July 15, 1986

Contents

PART THREE
WHEN THINGS ARE NOT
WHAT THEY SEEM

Editor's Foreword

The previous volumes in this series have dealt with formal matters: (1) issues of method or how we approach the interpretation of New Testament texts (form, redaction, and literary criticism, etc.), (2) questions of genre or literary type (proverb, letter, apocalypse, etc.); (3) questions of definition (What is New Testament theology?). The present volume continues this formal concern, although here, as earlier, formal questions have not been isolated from matters of content and meaning. This book is perhaps most closely akin to earlier ones that have dealt with various aspects of literary criticism. But rather than orienting itself to the application of modern literary approaches to the New Testament, it explores how ancient Jewish and Christian teachers and writers interpreted religious texts.

The Divinity School   DAN O. VIA
Duke University

given to a Jewish activity which finds its locus in the religious life of the Jewish community.[2] While others exegete their revelatory canons and while Jews exegete other texts, only Jews who explicitly tie their comments to the Bible engage in Midrash.[3]

Three elements are important in Porton's definition: (1) exegesis, (2) starting with Scripture, and (3) ending in community. Porton identifies five types of midrashic activity: the rabbinic (see part 3 of this book); the Midrash found in the Hebrew Scriptures themselves, for example, Deuteronomy's rewriting of Exodus, Numbers, and Leviticus; translations (Targumim); the rewriting of the biblical narrative; the Pesher-Midrash of an apocalyptic order. Porton writes as follows:

A further form of non-rabbinic Midrash from the turn of the eras is the rewriting of the biblical narrative. Such works as the *Liber Antiquitatum Biblicarum* of Pseudo-Philo, the *Genesis Apocryphon*, and *Jubilees* fall into this category. If we could establish that the early sections of Josephus' *Antiquities* and Philo's many allegories and his *Life of Moses* were written for communities which accepted the authority of the biblical texts upon which these writers built, these too could be fit into this category.

The *pesharim* found among the writings from Qumran represent yet another type of ancient Jewish Midrash, for its apocalyptic tone and its exclusive concern with the history of the Dead Sea Community set it apart from the other examples of ancient Jewish exegetical activity.[4]

Rabbinic Midrash is so called because it derives from the Judaic sages, who bear the honorific title of rabbis. While it is simply one more mode of biblical interpretation, it does exhibit traits of particular interest. Specifically, Porton surveys some of the internal technology that guides the rabbinic exegete in the reading of Scripture. The first point is that all details of a given verse of Scripture lay open for explanation and interpretation.

Every letter, every verse, and every phrase contained in the Bible was important and written as it was for a specific reason. The Bible contained no needless expressions, no "mere" repetitions, and no superfluous words or phrases. The assumption that every element of the biblical text was written in a specific way in order to teach something underlies the Midrashic activity of the rabbis.[5]

---

2. I distinguish between "midrash" and "exegesis" only by assigning the former word to activity within the Israelite community. It should be clear, however, that there may be extensive parallels between midrash which occurs within an Israelite context and exegesis which occurs in other religious and cultural systems.

3. For examples of the same rabbinic comments appearing as midrashic statements and non-midrashic statements, see Gary G. Porton, *Understanding Rabbinic Midrash: Texts and Commentary* (Hoboken, N.J.: Ktav, 1985), 6–8.

4. Porton, "Defining Midrash," 72.

5. Porton, *Understanding Rabbinic Midrash*, 9.

The advantage of relating one's comment on a verse to the character of that verse is simple. It bears the implication that what the exegete says now is the particular and inevitable message of the verse itself. Hence, this kind of Midrash, however fanciful, bears the claim of expressing the original meaning of Scripture — that is, God's meaning.

A second striking trait is the capacity to see relationships between one thing and something else, so Porton:

> Furthermore, the rabbis believed that everything contained in Scriptures was interrelated. Often, one verse is explained by reference to another verse. A section of the Prophets may be used to explain a verse from the Torah, or a portion of the Torah may explain a passage from the Writings.[6]

The search of the rabbinic sages was for the unity of human experience under God's rule. Hence they wanted to know what connections they could locate between scriptural stories, what lessons they could learn from one biblical teaching for the interpretation of another. Yet another trait, as Porton indicates, was an interest in showing the logical and reasonable character of divine revelation contained in Scripture. They wanted time and again to prove that reason without Scripture is not reliable, but that Scripture is reasonable:

> A common Midrashic activity is to refute a reasonable or logical conclusion merely by citing a verse from Scripture. The Midrashic activity was important, for without it, people might not act in proper ways and might misunderstand the realities of the world, man and God.[7]

These form some of the principal technical aspects of how sages read a verse of Scripture. As to the theological side to matters, Porton observes:

> A fifth assumption of the rabbis who engaged in the production of Midrash was that their activity was a religious, God-centered enterprise. While other peoples in Late Antiquity interpreted their ancient documents and even created many of the techniques which the rabbis used and which were codified in the lists of Midrashic rules attributed to Hillel, Ishmael, and Eliezer b. Yosi the Galilean, the rabbis alone believed that their activity was related to the word of the One and Only God. For the rabbis, the Hebrew Bible contained all the secrets of the universe, and it was the ultimate source of all knowledge and wisdom.
>   Rabbinic Midrash was thus one means of discovering these secrets, of attaining true knowledge and wisdom. The Bible was the only true guide for human action; it was the standard against which one measured one's deeds, the final arbiter of true and false, right and wrong. Rabbinic Midrash expounds only one document, and that text was not of human origin.[8]

6. Ibid.
7. Ibid.
8. Ibid., 10.

What makes the exegesis of Scripture, by Jews and Christians alike, different from the exegesis of Homer or Plato is the conviction of the exegetes that, through their reading they mediated God's Word to the world and so brought about salvation. That brings us to the diversity of this single and unitary venture: the types of Midrash-exegesis.

2

Three Dimensions of Midrash:
Exegesis, Document,
Process

The inquiry of *comparative midrash* — the foundation of the exposition of Midrash in this book — today encompasses three distinct activities, and in our inquiry into what Midrash is we shall undertake all three. People may mean that they wish to compare
1. processes or methods of exegesis of Scripture (e.g., hermeneutics),
2. compilations of exegeses of Scripture (i.e., whole documents), or
3. specific exegeses of a given verse of Scripture with other exegeses of the same verse.

When we compare, we first seek perspective on the things compared. Second, we look for the rule that applies to the unfamiliar thing among the things compared. The unknown thing is like something else, therefore falls under the rule governing the known thing to which it is likened, or it is unlike something else, therefore falls under the opposite rule.[1] Third, we compare so as to discover the context for interpreting the things compared. Through comparison we uncover traits that are unique to one thing as well as those that are shared among the things compared. Thus, we will survey several examples of Midrash and analyze their literary and programmatic traits (see parts 2 and 3).

In these three ways the labor of comparison and contrast forms the foundation of all inquiry into otherwise discrete and unintelligible data. Without perspective, knowledge of the applicable rule, and a conception of the context, we understand only the thing itself — and therefore nothing at all. For what is unique by definition is beyond comprehension. But what, precisely, do we compare when we compare midrash(im)? The answer will derive from asking how properly to com-

1. See G. E. R. Lloyd, *Polarity and Analogy. Two Types of Argumentation in Early Greek Thought* (Cambridge: Cambridge Univ. Press, 1966).

pare one thing with something else, in this case one midrash with another midrash. The reader will immediately wonder which of the three meanings I have adopted.

Do I mean comparing (1) the process, one mode of exegesis of Scripture with some other (e.g., comparing the methods of midrash-exegesis of Matthew with the methods of midrash-exegesis of the Dead Sea Scrolls)?

Do I mean (2) comparing the document or redactional and formulary plans and theological programs, the definitive traits of one compilation of exegeses with another such compilation (e.g., Matthew 2 with an equivalent composition of the Habakkuk commentary or with an equivalent passage of the *Sifré to Numbers*)?

Or do I mean comparing (3) the treatment of a given verse of Scripture-midrash in one compilation of exegeses-midrashim with the treatment of that same verse or theme of Scripture-midrash in another compilation of exegeses-midrashim?

Since the phrase "comparative midrash" has been applied to all three types of comparison, the answer to my question cannot emerge from common usage because common usage is confused. Here I propose to clarify and purify that usage!

I do so by arguing that, *to begin with,* the work of comparative midrash should commence with classification of compilations (2), and not classification of methods of exegesis of Scripture (1) occurring here, there, and everywhere, and also not with classification of discrete parts of documents (3). What should be compared at the outset is whole document to whole document, and only later of part of one document with part of another document, and last of all the exegetical approaches to one document with those of a second document.

Why should we begin and proceed this way? Because comparison begins in the definition of things that are to be compared. In short, we must know that things fall into a common genus, and only then shall we be able to ask how things are different from one another.

Therefore, in chapter 10 we compare Midrash-document to Midrash-document when we contrast Midrash-exegesis to Midrash-exegesis. That brings us to the importance of the document that contains a set of Midrash-exegeses of a passage or even whole book of Scripture. That document defines the framework of interest. Its editors have brought together various materials so as to make an overriding point, and much that they include in their document serves to register that point. Only when we know the impact of such a documentary context upon the materials in a document can we take up an individual item from that

14

document and set it into comparison and contrast with an item drawn out of some other document.

Why then must we first start with the definition of the documentary context, the compilation of exegeses (2)? The documentary context stands first in line because it rests upon the firmest premise: it is what we know for sure. No speculation whatever leads us to the claim that a given method of exegesis (1) has yielded a given exegetical comment (3) on a verse of Scripture, the result of which is now in our particular document (2). Since we know that simple fact — what is found in which document — we can begin the work of describing the traits imparted by that document to the exegetical result of the exegetical method at hand. Traits characteristic of the documentary setting likewise emerge without a trace of speculation. If a document routinely frames matters in accord with one repertoire of formal conventions rather than some other, and if it arranges its formal repertoire of types of units of discourse in one way rather than in some other, we can easily identify those traits of the passage under study that derive from the documentary context.

Accordingly, we begin with the whole document (2) because it presents the first solid fact. Everything else then takes a position relative to that fact. What then are some of the documentary facts? Here are some: this saying or story occurs here, bears these traits, is used for this larger redactional and programmatic purpose, makes this distinct point in its context, or no point at all. One may readily test these allegations and determine their facticity. These facts therefore define the initial context of interpretation. The facts deriving from the documentary setting define the context in which a given trait is shared or not shared among the two discrete items to be compared. One therefore does not begin by comparing methods of exegesis, or by comparing the exegesis of a verse in one document, deriving from one period and group of authorities, with the exegesis of that same verse in some other document, deriving from a completely different sort of authorities and a much earlier or later period. The results of such comparative work would be more information, but no interpretive insight.

I will now state my case negatively. If we ignore the characteristic traits of the documentary location(s) of an exegesis of a verse of Scripture or of a story occurring in two or more documents, then we do not know the rule governing both items subject to comparison. We establish no context that imparts meaning to the work of comparison. Why not? Because we have no perspective on similarities and differences among the two or more things that are to be compared. Similarities and differences may prove merely accidental. But we shall never know. Points of

15

likeness may constitute mere accidents of coincidence (e.g., of internal logic of the statement of the verse of Scripture at hand).

Now we turn to Midrash through the medium of the Midrash-compilations, examining each in turn and asking what we learn about Midrash in general from the ways in which people composed Midrash-compilations — and therefore also created Midrash-exegeses on the basis of the Midrash-processes they found self-evidently persuasive. Since all Midrash begins in Scripture, we start with an account of what all later exegetes in Judaism learned *through* Scripture about correct interpretation *of* Scripture. For, as all exegetes concur, Scripture forms its own best interpretation. On that basis, all of us in the world of the Hebrew Bible undertake the exercise of disciplined interpretation. We bring our questions to find Scripture's answers and we follow Scripture's example in our search: Midrash as method begins in the Hebrew Bible itself.

3

Midrash within the Hebrew Scriptures

By its very character—topic, rhetoric, and logic of cogent discourse—a document that we choose to interpret dictates to us the shape and structure of our interpretation: the topics and the kinds of questions we can address to those topics. In this sense all exegesis originates in the text itself! There is, however, a second sense in which the Hebrew Scriptures inaugurated the process of their own interpretation. Specifically, the Scriptures unfold in such a way that one document—a passage or a whole book—responds to an earlier one. We observe the simple fact that exegesis of Scripture was routine and ubiquitous even in the times in which various books of the Hebrew Bible were coming into being. To understand Midrash-exegesis one begins with the very Scripture that is subjected to exegesis. This fact—that the Hebrew Scripture contains the antecedents for later Jewish biblical exegesis—is stated clearly by Michael Fishbane:

. . . the broad range of stylistic patterns from many periods, together with their corresponding technical terms, strategies or procedures, suggest that exegetical techniques and traditions developed locally and cumulatively in ancient Israel from monarchic times and continued into the Graeco-Roman period, where they served as a major reservoir for the Jewish schools and techniques of exegesis then developing . . .[1]

True, Fishbane qualifies that judgment, maintaining that these materials "only suggest trajectories of exegetical tradition over the course of centuries; the evidence is insufficient to prove historical dependence." So Fishbane states:

1. Michael Fishbane, *Biblical Interpretation in Ancient Israel* (Oxford: Clarendon Press, 1985), 525.

. . . the texts and traditions . . . were not simply copied, studied, transmitted, or recited. They were also . . . subject to redaction, elucidation, reformulation, and outright transformation. Accordingly, our received traditions are complex blends of *traditium* and *traditio* in dynamic interaction, dynamic interpenetration, and dynamic interdependence.[2]

Midrash begins in Scripture, and the later masters of Midrash-exegesis derived models for their task from Scripture itself.

Those familiar with the documentary hypothesis on the Pentateuch, with its components known as J, E, JE, P, and D, will recall, for example, how the authorship of Deuteronomy has taken over materials of Exodus, Numbers, and parts of Leviticus, and reworked those materials in a fresh and interesting way. An earlier formulation may be subjected to amplification, expansion, reworking, or rewording. The Ten Commandments in Exodus (Exod. 20:2–17) and in Deuteronomy (Deut. 5:6–21) contain different versions of the same matter, for example:

Remember the sabbath day,   Observe the sabbath day,
to keep it holy.   to keep it holy,
    as the Lord your God commanded you.

Differences in wording yield little exegetical material. But while Exodus invokes the creation of the world, Deuteronomy appeals to the exodus from Egypt.

Exodus

For in six days the Lord made heaven and earth, the sea, and all that is in them, and rested the seventh day; therefore the Lord blessed the sabbath day and hallowed it.

Deuteronomy

You shall remember that you were a servant in the land of Egypt, and the Lord your God brought you out thence with a mighty hand and an outstretched arm; therefore the Lord your God commanded you to keep the sabbath day.

Differences in Scripture itself, such as these, demand exegesis and also define the exegetical task. Scholars today may explain these differences in historical terms; exegetes in times past, as today, bring a different set of questions. But in this and many other ways, Scripture defines the work to be done by Midrash and also suggests how that work will be carried out.

Not only so, but Scripture itself contains examples of how one writer received and amplified the work of a prior set of writers. A simple

2. Ibid., 543.

instance of the so-called internal-biblical exegetical mode, for example, is given by a contrast of Ps. 106:32–33 and Num. 20:2–13. The former of the two passages supplies a motive for the action described in the latter. We begin with the story, as narrated at Num. 20:10–13.

And Moses and Aaron gathered the assembly together before the rock, and he said to them, "Hear now, you rebels; shall we bring forth water for you out of this rock?" And Moses lifted up his hand and struck the rock with his rod twice; and water came forth abundantly, and the congregation drank, and their cattle. And the Lord said to Moses and Aaron, "Because you did not believe in me, to sanctify me in the eyes of the people of Israel, therefore you shall not bring this assembly into the land which I have given them." These are the waters of Meribah, where the people of Israel contended with the Lord, and he showed himself holy among them.

Why then did Moses strike the rock? The foregoing account at best suggests an implicit motive for his action. The author of Ps. 106:32–33 makes it explicit:

They angered him at the waters of Meribah, and it went ill with Moses on their account; for they made his spirit bitter, and he spoke words that were rash.

The psalmist has answered the question, why did Moses hit the rock? That was left open in the story. Now what is important in this instance is simply the evidence of how, within the pages of the Hebrew Scriptures, a program of exegesis (now called Midrash) reaches full exposure.

Furthermore, we need not hunt at length for evidence of the work of collecting such exercises in exegesis — of rewriting an old text in light of new considerations or values. Such a vast enterprise is illustrated by Chronicles: instead of merely commenting on verses the chronicler actually rewrites the stories of Samuel and Kings. One has not paid attention to the full documentary context if one compares what the compilers of Samuel and Kings say about a given incident with what the compilers of Chronicles say about the same; one misses the point of the difference between the reading of the one and that of the other. The difference derives from the documentary context, there alone! Without asking, first of all, about the plan and program of the documents, the formal comparison of contents produces facts or information but no insight into their meaning.

The chronicler, working alongside Ezra and Nehemiah, taught lessons to the people of his time drawn from the history of the people and is called "a Midrashist."[3] The chronicler reworked Deuteronomy, Joshua,

3. Jacob M. Myers, *II Chronicles*, Anchor Bible (Garden City, N.Y.: Doubleday & Co., 1965), xx.

Judges, Samuel, and Kings. Time and again, as Myers comments.[4] "As always, the Chronicler is interested chiefly in the theological aspects of the story. This is the sermon of the writer informing his hearers of the reason for exile and at the same time pointing out the plan of Yahweh in which they are participants. . . . Thus Jerusalem was destroyed, the temple leveled, and the people taken into exile because of the wrath of Yahweh kindled by the refusal of king and officials to listen to his word." Thus here the chronicler reworks received materials. He does not cite a verse and then comment. Rather he rewrites the received materials to make his points.

Obviously, neither of these two biblical cases — exegesis by implicit rereading of a story, exegesis by implicit rewriting of a set of received stories — exhausts the range of the Scriptures' own Midrash. Both serve merely to provide instances of the antiquity of both making up and also purposefully compiling exegeses of Scripture. They call into question any notion that a distinctive historical circumstance — that of late antiquity, for example — frames the context in which we are to read all works of Midrash-exegesis of Scripture.

When people wished to deliver a powerful argument for a basic proposition, they did so by collecting and arranging exegeses of Scripture and also by producing appropriate exegeses of Scripture for these compilations. That is, compilers also participated in the framing or rewriting of what they compiled, so that all we have is what they chose to give us in the language and form they selected. Thus I maintain that study of Midrash must always entail proper comparison. That comparison ordinarily begins with the character of the compilation of exegeses. Comparing one compilation with another then defines the first stage of the comparison of exegeses.

We now turn to Midrash-exegesis and Midrash-compilations that took the two forms of paraphrase and prophecy, respectively: translations of Scripture and reading of scriptural passages in light of current events. Only when we have seen this approach at work shall we understand what is distinctive about the midrashic enterprise created by the Judaic sages of the dual Torah.

4. Ibid., 222.

TWO TYPES OF MIDRASH AMONG ANCIENT JUDAISMS

4

Paraphrase: Midrash in the Septuagint and the Targumim*

By rendering Scripture into another language, the translator makes a statement not only upon, but also of, the meaning of Scripture. And that statement falls into the category of Midrash, meaning in this case "paraphrase." For a translation by its nature presents a paraphrase of the original, since, moving from one language to another, one cannot present a meaningful statement merely by putting down the equivalent in one language of a word of another. As computer translations show, that kind of word-for-word translation often yields gibberish. In antiquity people understood that fact and when they translated, they also accomplished a labor of interpretation of a highly creative and original order. The Hebrew Scriptures were translated into two languages, Greek and Aramaic, because Jews in large numbers spoke those languages in the Greco-Roman world and, in the case of Aramaic, in the Iranian world as well. Hence they received the revelation of Sinai in the vernacular as they knew it.

The translation of the Pentateuch into Old Greek (Septuagint or LXX) began in the third century B.C.E.[1] Produced for educational and possibly also liturgical uses of Egyptian Jews by Alexandrian Jewish translators, the LXX provides "translations" rather than a "translation." The translation into Old Greek was an extended process continuing for

---

*The discussion of the Septuagint was written by Ernest S. Frerichs and revised by me; that on the Targumim was written by Paul V. Flesher and revised by me.

1. For a Septuagint studies bibliography, see S. F. Brock et al., *A Classified Bibliography of the Septuagint* (Leiden: E. J. Brill, 1973), and the annual *Bulletin* of the International Organization for Septuagint and Cognate Studies. Studies on translation and related issues can be found in H. B. Swete, ed., *Introduction to the Old Testament in Greek*, 2d ed. (New York: Macmillan, 1902); S. Jellicoe, *The Septuagint and Modern Study* (New York and London: Oxford Univ. Press, 1968); S. Jellicoe, ed., *Studies in the Septuagint: Origins, Recensions and Interpretations* (New York: Ktav, 1974); L. Prijs, *Jüdische Tradition in der Septuaginta* (Leiden: E. J. Brill, 1948); E. Tov, *The Text-Critical Use of the Septuagint in Biblical Research* (Jerusalem: Simor, 1981).

a considerable period after the initial translation of the Pentateuch and carried on in Alexandria and possibly Palestine. By the first century C.E. it is already possible to find quotations and allusions from the Septuagint in Philo, Josephus, and the NT Paul.

The translators had no models. So they had to make decisions on what their translation(s) would accomplish. The choices before them depended upon how they classified the Hebrew Scriptures. Was the Bible as they received it to be viewed as a legal document in which the translator strives to convey the exact meaning of the original text through a "literal" translation? Or was it to be viewed as a literary text permitting the use of "free" or paraphrastic translation? If the translation was to provide a basis for claiming it as "inspired," the admission of paraphrastic translation was already a potential obstacle. The view that the Pentateuch was both legal and literary resulted in a translation which was both literal and free. Beyond the classification of the text being translated, the translators also needed to take into account the relative prestige of Hebrew and Greek in the areas in which the translation would be used as well as the degree to which Hebrew was actually known in the areas of LXX usage.

What is a close rendering? Ralph Marcus observed that "every translation is a compromise between two civilizations."[2] One-to-one correspondences between the words of one language and the apparent counterpart word of another language are nonexistent. Marcus provides a persuasive simile: "A translated word or phrase more nearly resembles a mature immigrant who speaks the language of his adopted country with a different accent, different associations and different inner responses from those of the native." Despite their fidelity to the scriptural text, the translators of the Pentateuch produced a Midrash, the effects of which would have continuing influence on the subsequent exegetical work of both Jews and Christians. This achievement was effected primarily through such means as paraphrastic translations to secure an idiomatic rendering and interpretative additions, deletions, or reorderings of the text. It is the very presence of such elements in translation that force the student of LXX translations to recognize the problem of reconstructing the Hebrew text(s) used by the translators. In those instances in which the LXX text differs from the received or Masoretic Text, it may have been because of a different Hebrew text, but it may also have resulted from the translation style, or tendential concerns, or the attempt to harmonize parallel passages. It must also be said that on

2. Ralph Marcus, "Jewish and Greek Elements in the Septuagint," in *Louis Ginzberg Jubilee Volume* (Philadelphia: Jewish Publication Society of America, 1945), 1:229.

occasion the differences may be explicable in terms of the inability to resolve problems of the Hebrew text. Whatever the nature of the specific Hebrew text before the translators, it would have been in the form of a consonantal text requiring vocalization. The vocalization provided further opportunity for error in vocalization, for choice between homophonous forms, and for midrashic reflections in translating the text. Such considerations could lead the LXX translators to translate a Hebrew name into a Greek name reflecting the meaning of the name, and not just a transliterated form, as in the translation of the name "Eve" (ḤWH) with the Greek "Zoē." There are numerous instances in which the Greek translators sought to remove embarrassing references to strong and positive figures in the biblical tradition. Judges 18:30, for instance, tells us of the action of the Danites in erecting an idol in their city. The text goes on to note that Jonathan, a grandson of Moses, and Jonathan's sons became priests to the Danites. In these instances the Hebrew text was changed by introducing the Hebrew letter nun into the Hebrew text and "Moses" (MŠH) became "Manasseh" (MNŠH). The evidence for this is in the LXX reading which renders "Moses" with "Manasseh." Theological considerations influenced translations and certainly did so in the case of the LXX. The Hebrew text of Exod. 24:10 tells us that "they [Moses and those with him] saw the God of Israel." Seeing the Deity directly was a serious issue for ancient Israel and the LXX provided a translation in which "they saw *the place where* the God of Israel *stood*." This same concern is seen in the LXX translation of Isa. 38:11 in which the LXX has modified the Hebrew text where King Hezekiah says "I shall not see the Lord in the land of the living" to "I shall not see *the salvation of* the Lord." This type of translation does not represent problems with the Hebrew of the text before the translators, whether from scribal error in transmission or in differences in the Hebrew text itself. It is most easily understood as an attempt to convey in Greek solutions to problems which were clearly recognized in the religious assumptions of ancient Israel.

Paraphrastic readings were often secured by glosses through which the translators introduced a word or words into the text. Some of these glosses seek only to explain. Others reflect differing readings of the text. Still others may be best understood as expressions of traditional religious sentiment. The LXX translation of the Book of Proverbs, a later translation and usually classified as a "free" translation, provides ample evidence for glossing activity by the Greek translators. In Prov. 1:7, for example, we read: "The fear of the Lord is the beginning of knowledge;

25

but fools scorn wisdom and discipline." The LXX translators provide a faithful translation of the verse, but preface the verse with a quote from Ps. 111:10: "The fear of the Lord is the beginning of wisdom; those who practice it have sound sense." On occasion laws of the Pentateuch will be given clarification by the LXX translators. In Exod. 22:8, for example, "the owner of the house shall come near to God," has been enlarged by the LXX translator to include "and shall swear." Exodus 22:29 provides a further example of this form of paraphrastic exegesis. The Hebrew text speaks of "your abundance and your juice," but the LXX translators have provided a translation which speaks of "the first fruits of your threshing floor and wine press." The modern study of the translation style of the LXX translators is still in its early stages, but increasing attention is being paid to the Greek Bible in its own right and not only as a means of understanding the Hebrew Bible. We have, however, learned to recognize approaches to translation that are clearly midrashic as well as to identify exegeses familiar to us from later rabbinic texts.

The problem facing the translators of Scripture into Aramaic — that is, the translators who produced the Targum(s) — was no different, but the medium was. For Aramaic is far closer to Hebrew than is Greek. The word "Targum" means "translation." The Targums were composed by Jews, some in Galilee, others in Babylonia, sometime between 300 and 700 c.e.[3] The Targums contain material that predates the composition of the document as a whole. There are three complete Targums to the Pentateuch: *Targum Onkelos, Targum Neofiti*, and *Targum Pseudo-Jonathan*. These Targums vary in the amount of midrashic material they contain: *Onkelos* contains the least while *Pseudo-Jonathan* has the most. There is only one Targum to the Prophets: *Targum Jonathan*. It contains translations of most of the prophetic, historical, and wisdom books of the Hebrew Scriptures.[4] The Aramaic translations of the Hebrew Scriptures undertake two modes of Midrash-exegesis. First, the translators so paraphrase the original Hebrew as to alter its meaning and impute a new and rich sense. Second, in the guise of translation the authors insert quite fresh materials — interpretations of the given or

3. There is evidence that there were Aramaic translations dating earlier than 300 c.e. For example, fragments of a targum to Leviticus were found at Qumran (therefore dating prior to 66 c.e.). Archaeologists also found an Aramaic version of the story of Abraham and Sarah in Egypt, now called *The Genesis Apocryphon*. It rewrites rather than translates the Genesis story, and so is not, strictly speaking, a strict targum. Documents of formative Judaism, such as the *Mishnah*, also mention written targums, especially a targum to Job which does not exist today.

4. There are no good, up-to-date, introductions to the Targums. In English, the best is M. McNamara, *Targum and Testament* (Grand Rapids: Wm. B. Eerdmans, 1972). In French, the classic introduction is R. Le Déaut, *Introduction à la Littérature Targumique* (Rome: Pontifical Biblical Institute, 1966).

details made up for the occasion — into their presentation of the original Hebrew. In these two ways they enrich the received account and create Midrash-exegesis, producing the Midrash-document comprised by their Targum.

The reason that the Midrash as paraphrase emerged from the labor of translation from Hebrew to the more commonly known Aramaic is simple. Linguistically, Aramaic — unlike the Greek of the Septuagint — is very similar to Hebrew. The two languages possess the same grammatical, syntactical, and semantic structures. Thus, when Hebrew is translated into Aramaic, it can be done in a word-for-word manner to reflect both the word order of the original and its grammatical and syntactic elements. In the Targums, therefore, the Midrash-process defined by paraphrase — restating the sense of a text in other words — guides the translator as he states his ideas in the language and structure of his translation of Scripture. In doing this, the targumist produces a fairly accurate translation of the Hebrew text that he keeps in its original sequence. The targumist works in his own issues by adding onto the translation those words and phrases that express his point. He rarely obliterates his translation of the Hebrew text. He simply augments it, sometimes with only a word or two, at other times with so much additional material that the original is almost unrecognizable.

Our examples of Midrash as paraphrase are taken from *Targum Neofiti*, the earliest complete Targum in hand. The first passage demonstrates two points about translation and Midrash as paraphrase in Targums. First, the Aramaic translation is an almost word-for-word equivalent of the original Hebrew text. Second, the targumist makes his point here by altering just one word of the translation. For clarity, we have translated the two texts into English to reflect both the similarities and differences found in the original two languages,[5] dividing the passages into clauses and numbering them so that the parallels are more readily apparent.

1. Observe the words of this covenant,
2. and perform them,
3. so that you act wisely in all that you do.
   (Deut. 29:9 [Heb. 29:8])

1. And observe the words of this *praiseworthy Torah*
2. and perform them,
3. so that you act wisely in all that you do.
   (*Targum Neofiti* to Deut. 29:9[8])

5. All translations of Scripture and *Targum Neofiti* in this chapter have been made by Paul Flesher.

First, when we compare lines 2 and 3 in the original with the same lines in the Targum, we see that the Aramaic directly reproduces the Hebrew text. It is a word-for-word translation of the original. Second, line 1 in *Neofiti* is not an exact translation of the Hebrew. The targumist introduces an important change which alters the meaning of the verse, namely the change of "covenant" in the Hebrew to "Torah" in the Aramaic. In the Hebrew text, v. 9 constitutes an exhortation to obey the laws and commandments contained in the "covenant" between God and Israel, which the preceding chapters of Deuteronomy have just spelled out. By substituting "Torah" for "covenant," the targumist makes this instruction refer not just to the body of laws just described, but to the whole collection of law and lore designated by the term "Torah." For the Judaism practiced in the time this Targum was composed (say 400 C.E.), "Torah" signified the traditions and laws contained in both the written and the oral Torah, a much broader corpus than that indicated by "covenant." Here we can see how the targumist accomplished his Midrash-exegesis with little disruption to the exact translation of the original text and still altered the verse to reflect his own point.

Another way in which Midrash as paraphrase occurs is in a close translation of the Hebrew text. The targumist translates a whole verse word-for-word, but by introducing his Midrash through the addition of four words, he completely alters the point of the verse. An example of this is Gen. 2:15:

1. And the Lord God took the man
2. and caused him to rest in the Garden of Eden,
3. to work it
4. and to keep it.

(Gen. 2:15)

1. And the Lord God took the man
2. and caused him to dwell in the Garden of Eden
3. in order to work *in the Torah* [*i.e., to study*]
4. and to keep its *commandments.*
(*Targum Neofiti* to Gen. 2:15)

The targumist has performed an exact translation of the verse. But in lines 3 and 4 he has added a couple words that completely alter the point of the verse and therefore of the whole story of the Garden of Eden. In the original text, God puts Adam in the garden to act as a gardener; he is "to work it and to keep it." Thus, man's original task is to farm. But the targumist changes that occupation merely by adding four words, namely, "the Torah" in line 3 and "its commandments" in line 4. The Targum now indicates that Adam's archetypal occupation is that of a Torah sage. He is supposed to study Torah and to perform the tasks it requires. Thus man's primary function is to "do" Torah, both by study and by performance of its commandments. By paraphrasing the original text, the targumist introduces his Midrash on the text.

The targumist of *Targum Neofiti* completely rewrites the story of Adam's fall in the Garden of Eden. In each part of the story where important action takes place, he introduces the issue of Torah study and practice. Accordingly, the verse where God curses the snake for his part in Adam's downfall provides the targumist an important place for his Midrash as paraphrase. In this case, the Midrash is much larger than the translated verse, instead of being just a small proportion as in the previous two examples. Despite this fact, the targumist still places his Midrash within the structure of the original text.

1. I will put hostility between you and the woman,
2. and between your seed and her seed.
3. He shall bruise your head
4. and you shall bruise his heel.

(Gen. 3:15)

1. And I will put hostility between you and the woman,
2. and between your children and her children.
3. *And when her children guard the Torah and keep the commandments they will aim against you and* strike you on your head *and kill you.*
4. *And when they forsake the commandments of the Torah, you will take aim and* bite them on their heels *and cause them to sicken.*
5. *However, there will be a cure for her children, but for you there will be no cure. For in the future they will find relief in the Remnant [of Israel?] in the day of the King Messiah.*

(Targum Neofiti to Gen. 3:15)

The first two phrases of the Hebrew text are accurately reproduced in the Aramaic. But the targumist takes great liberty with phrases 3 and 4. In Scripture, the snake's offspring and the woman's offspring are balanced; each shall injure the other. There is no condition for ending the conflict nor any indication that one side will overcome the other. The targumist, by contrast, makes the whole conflict dependent on the actions of human beings. When people study and practice Torah, they are victorious over the snake. When they cease to study and practice, they let the snake get the upper hand. The targumist makes these points within the structure set by the Hebrew verse. He simply translates the verse—at lines 3 and 4—and adds his point around the translation. At phrase 5, he concludes his point by stating that in the end, human beings will have the upper hand. This phrase is not a paraphrase of a part of the text, but it concludes the argument that makes up the para-

29

phrase in lines 3 and 4. So, although it is not a paraphrase of the verse, it forms part of the Midrash that the targumist chooses to put on the verse.

So far we have seen how the point of a verse is changed. The targumist introduces his own issues and paraphrases them through the course of his translation. The following passage carries this process one step further. Here, the translation states the exact opposite point of the Hebrew text.

1. How should one pursue a thousand,
2. and two cause a myriad to flee,
3. if their Rock (i.e., God] had not sold them,
4. and the Lord had given them up?
> (Deut. 32:30)

1. *When Israel used to work in the Torah* [*i.e., study*] *and kept its commandments,*
2. one *of them used to* pursue a thousand,
3. and two of them used to cause myriad *of myriads* to flee.
4. *But because they sinned and brought about wrath before Him,*
5. *the Strong One* [i.e., God] has forsaken them
6. *and the* memra [word] *of the Lord has delivered them into the hands of their enemies.*
> (*Targum Neofiti* to Deut. 32:30)

When the Hebrew text talks of "a thousand" and "a myriad," it refers to Israelites who are being pursued by their enemies. The reason for their extreme weakness and faintheartedness is that God has forsaken them. The targumist completely changes the sense. In the Targum (lines 1–3), the Israelites are the pursuers who were made strong because of their study and practice of the Torah. It is not Israel's enemies who were strong but the people of Israel themselves. Note how the targumist accomplishes this switch. He translates the opening two lines of the Hebrew fairly accurately in the Targum's second and third lines, but he adds an introductory clause (line 1). This introduction changes the context — specifically, it states that these feats of strength come from the Torah, not from God's forsaking of the Israelites, which is the point of the Hebrew text. Lines 4–6 of the Targum are constructed in a similar manner. The opening line, phrase 4, is added, while 5 and 6 constitute a paraphrastic translation of phrases 3 and 4 of the Hebrew. Line 4 of the Targum makes it clear that God has forsaken the Israelites because of their sin, not — as might be implied by the Hebrew — for no reason at all.

30

5

Prophecy: Midrash in the
Dead Sea Scrolls*

Midrash as prophecy tells us that in Scripture we find accounts
of the meaning of what is happening and what is going to happen. The
Essenes, who constituted an Israelite monastic community and lived in
a commune at Wadi Qumran, a mile or so from the Dead Sea, present
us with one striking example of reading Scripture verse by verse: as
prophecy, an exegetical way of transforming the past into a statement
concerning the present and future.[1] The Essenes founded their community sometime in the second century B.C.E. and occupied it, off and on,
until it was destroyed by the Romans in 66 C.E. The Essenes' view of
their own history — gleaned from the hints and clues in their writings —
runs something like this. Early in the second century B.C.E., the Essenes
were merely groups of extremely pious Israelites who lived in the cities
and villages of Judah. This group was led by priests who emphasized
their descent from David's high priest, Zadok, and consisted of members
of the three main castes, priests, Levites, and Israelites. Like most Israelites at the time, they believed that the Temple in Jerusalem constituted
the focus of the worship of Yahweh, the God of Israel. As such, it must
be kept sacred and holy and free from any contamination. The Essene
groups had one distinctive belief, however — that the high priest of the
Temple must be a descendant of the line of Zadok. At some point in the

---

* Co-authored with Paul Flesher.
1. The best guide to the Qumran community are the translated documents, with introduction by
G. Vermes, *The Dead Sea Scrolls in English*, 2d ed. (Baltimore and Harmondsworth: Penguin Books,
1975). See also his handbook on the state of scholarship: *The Dead Sea Scrolls: Qumran in Perspective*,
rev. ed. (Philadelphia: Fortress Press, 1981). See also the bibliographic guide of Joseph A. Fitzmyer, *The
Dead Sea Scrolls: Major Publications and Tools for Study* (Missoula, Mont.: Scholars Press, 1979). See
the recent studies on pesherim by Maurya P. Horgan, *Pesherim: Qumran Interpretations of Biblical
Books* (Washington, D.C.: Catholic Biblical Association of America, 1979), and William H. Brownlee,
The Midrash Pesher of Habakkuk (Missoula, Mont.: Scholars Press, 1979).

middle of the second century, a priest with improper lineage became the high priest (perhaps one of the Hasmoneans). This represented a major disaster to the Essenes. To them, it meant that the Temple was violated and defiled. The false high priest rendered the Temple an abomination to God, and therefore unsuited for worship of Yahweh. Shortly thereafter, this high priest persecuted the members of the Essene groups. They fled their homes and eventually congregated at Qumran.

To understand the world view brought by Essene-Judaism to Scripture, we turn to its principal figure and his concern. The leader of the Essenes was called the Teacher of Righteousness. He was a pious and holy man, apparently a priestly descendant of Zadok. He organized the Qumran community and unlocked the secrets of the prophets to them. He revealed to them that they were living in the end of days predicted by the Israelite prophets. Soon, God would crush God's enemies in a final cosmic battle and usher in the new age of righteousness. The Essenes themselves were the last remnant of the true Israel. As such, they would play a leading role in the final battle. They would emerge victorious from it and return to Jerusalem to purify the Temple and to reinstitute the proper worship of Yahweh. When they read Scripture, the Essenes brought with them a sizable corpus of factual knowledge, in light of which they interpreted what they read.

The Essenes included in their library manuals describing the discipline of the community, collections of hymns, descriptions of the last days of the age, and exegetical works. It is these last documents that draw our interest. Scholars call these texts "pesharim" (sing. "pesher"), which means "interpretation" in Hebrew. Each of these texts constitutes a Midrash — an interpretation — on a prophetical book from Scripture. Archaeologists have found fragments of commentaries to the Books of Isaiah, Nahum, Hosea, Micah, and Habakkuk, as well as to Psalm 37.

The forms of Midrash in the Dead Sea Scrolls reveal to us a sustained effort to identify contemporary events with the scriptural prophetic passages of the past. The self-evident purpose of the exegete is to allow for further inquiry into the near future. For once Scripture has made its statement about the future that the later exegete thinks has taken place, the exegete finds solid ground for listening for yet further messages from the same scriptural prophetic passages. The Midrash-compilations (see chap. 2) in the category of *Midrash as prophecy* demonstrate the unity of form and meaning, of purpose and proposition. These definitive traits of Midrash — the selection of exegeses, the creation of exegeses, the arrangement and compilation of exegeses, the use of a particular formal technique, and the larger polemic or theological proposition that motivated the compilers and exegetes alike—all join in producing the remarkable Essene-Judaic Midrash.

As presented by Geza Vermes[2] the exegeses do seem to form a collection, or at least a chapter, that is, a systematic treatment of a number of verses in sequence.

Commentary on Hosea

In this interpretation, the unfaithful wife is the Jewish people, and her lovers are the Gentiles who have led the nation astray.

[She knew not that] it was I who gave her [the new wine and oil], who lavished [upon her silver] and gold which they [used for Baal] (ii, 8).

Interpreted, this means that [they ate and] were filled, but they forgot God who . . . They cast His commandments behind them which He had sent [by the hand of] His servants the Prophets, and they listened to those who led them astray. They revered them, and in their blindness they feared them as though they were gods.

Therefore I will take back my corn in its time and my wine [in its season]. I will take away my wool and my flax lest they cover [her nakedness]. I will uncover her shame before the eyes of [her] lovers [and] no man shall deliver her from out of my hand (ii, 9-10).

Interpreted, this means that He smote them with hunger and nakedness that they might be shamed and disgraced in the sight of the nations on which they relied. They will not deliver them from their miseries.

I will put an end to her rejoicing, [her feasts], her [new] moons, her Sabbaths, and all her festivals (ii, 11).

Interpreted, this means that [they have rejected the ruling of the law, and have] followed the festivals of the nations. But [their rejoicing shall come to an end and] shall be changed into mourning.

I will ravage [her vines and her fig trees], of which she said, "They are my wage [which my lovers have given me."] I will make of them a thicket and the [wild beasts] shall eat them . . . (ii, 12).

The interpreter's focus on a single point is striking in the Midrash of the pesharim. The scriptural prophetic writer (e.g., Hosea) is interpreted as referring to the Essene community of Qumran and the events that surround it. In other words, in the commentator's view, the prophets prophesied about the Essenes. From our standpoint, this means that the Qumran interpreter understands the prophetic text to be referring to something which, on the surface, it is not. The Qumran interpreter tries to identify the hidden meaning and make it clear.

Another Midrash-commentary proceeds sequentially through the Book of Habakkuk. First, the writer quotes a section of Scripture (e.g., a prophet) and then interprets that section. He then proceeds to the next portion of Scripture, interprets it, and so on. In this manner, the exegete

---

2. Vermes, Dead Sea Scrolls in English, 230.

proceeds step by step through the scriptural text; he does not skip around in the text, saying something about this passage but not that one. Second, despite the verse-commentary-verse-commentary organization of the pesher, each commentary does not focus solely on the preceding verse. Indeed, the commentator performs an extended dialogue with the scriptural prophetic text and through that dialogue makes his points. The example below constitutes an ongoing discussion about the Wicked Priest, a discussion which begins with Hab. 2:15 and is carried on in v. 16 and, as we shall see in a moment, in v. 17. Third, each of the interpretations (pesharim) treat the whole biblical verse. Despite this, certain elements of the scriptural passage are reflected in the interpretation. Habakkuk's "venom" becomes the pesher's "venomous fury" while the "you" indicates the "Wicked Priest" and "to make them drunk" is reflected in "to confuse them, and to cause them to stumble."

The interpretation of Hab. 2:17 carries forward the comments on the preceding two verses and spells out even more of the Priest's wicked deeds for which God will punish him, as the Dead Sea Scrolls indicate:

[*For the violence done to Lebanon shall overwhelm you, and the destruction of the beasts*] *shall terrify you, because of the blood of men and the violence done to the land, the city, and all its inhabitants* (ii, 17).
Interpreted, this saying concerns the Wicked Priest, inasmuch as he shall be paid the reward which he himself tendered to the Poor. For *Lebanon* is the Council of the Community; and the *beasts* are the Simple of Judah who keep the Law. As he himself plotted the destruction of the Poor, so will God condemn him to destruction. And as for that which He said, *Because of the blood of the city and the violence done to the land:* interpreted, *the city* is Jerusalem where the Wicked Priest committed abominable deeds and defiled the Temple of God. *The violence done to the land:* these are the cities of Judah where he robbed the Poor of their possessions.[3]

This interpretation carries forward the comments on vv. 15 and 16; the writer delineates how the ancient scriptural prophetic text speaks of the Wicked Priest and the actions against the Qumran community. Now the commentator selects individual words from the scriptural passage and interprets them on their own. He treats them like a symbolic code and attempts to unlock the identity of each one. First, the commentator identifies the "you" of the prophetic text with the Wicked Priest. The interpreter identifies the next two nouns of the scriptural text, "Lebanon" and "the beasts," as the leaders of the Qumran community and the community itself. "The Poor" and "the Simple" apparently constitute

3. Ibid., 242.

names by which the sectarians refer to themselves. "The city" of Scripture is then identified as Jerusalem where the Wicked Priest has defiled the Temple and "the land" refers to the towns where the Essenes once had lived. In this way, the sectarian writer decodes the scriptural prophet and shows how his remarks foretell the events surrounding the Essene community.

The Essene sages furthermore applied this method of exegesis to the books of the Pentateuch, as is the case in *The Damascus Rule*, the manual of discipline for the community. The Midrash focuses on Num. 21:18. In Numbers, this verse comprises a brief song that is placed into a larger, narrative section. No prophecy occurs in the scriptural text. But this does not prevent the Essene commentator from interpreting the text as if it were prophecy:

> But God remembered the Covenant with the forefathers, and He raised from Aaron men of discernment and from Israel men of wisdom, and He caused them to hear. And they dug the Well: *the well which the princes dug, which the nobles of the people delved with the stave* (Num. xxi, 18)
> The *Well* is the Law, and those who dug it were the converts of Israel who went out of the land of Judah to sojourn in the land of Damascus. God called them all *princes* because they sought Him, and their renown was disputed by no man. The *Stave* is the Interpreter of the Law of whom Isaiah said, *He makes a tool for His work* (Isa. liv, 16); and *the nobles of the people* are those who come to dig the *Well* with the staves with which the *Stave* ordained that they should walk in all the age of wickedness — and without them they shall find nothing — until he comes who shall teach righteousness at the end of days.[4]

The commentator decodes key words and phrases, and identifies their equivalents. The "well" is the Law (i.e., Scripture), "the princes" are the Qumran community, and the "Stave" can only be the Teacher of Righteousness who interpreted and explained the true meaning of Scripture to the community. According to the passage's final sentence, the Teacher's interpretation constitutes the sole true understanding until the eschatological end of time. Thus we can see that Midrash as prophecy works in the same way for nonprophetic portions of Scripture as well as for the prophetic. In both cases it wants to show that ancient Scripture really refers to the Qumran community and its situation at the end of time.

What we have in Essene Midrash-compilations therefore is an entirely cogent Midrash-exegesis comprising a Midrash-document that expresses a Midrash-process, namely, an approach to the verses of Scripture in

4. Ibid., 102–3.

light of an available correlation of concrete events to past words. The exegete relates to Scripture things that have happened in his own day. Why?

The framer of the passage selected a mode of constructing his unit of discourse wholly congruent with the purpose for which, to begin with, he undertook the exegesis of the passage.

He wished to read the verses of Scripture in light of events. So he organized his unit of discourse around the sequence of verses of Scripture under analysis. Had he wanted, he might have provided a sequential narrative of what happened, then inserted the verse he found pertinent, thus: "X happened, and that is the meaning of (biblical verse) Y." (Such a mode of organizing exegeses served the school of Matthew, but not the framer of the Essene text. I do not know why.) In any event the construction at hand is rather simple.

The far more complex modes of constructing units of discourse that we shall meet in *Genesis Rabbah* and *Leviticus Rabbah* served a different purpose. They are made up, moreover, of different approaches to the exegesis of Scripture. In short, the exegete's purpose affects not only the content of an exegetical appropriation of another text from another document but also the editorial shape of the document he creates with the accumulation of such exegetical appropriations.

It may now be argued that the rather episodic sets of exegeses presented to us by the Essene library of Qumran cannot be called documents when they are compared to the sustained and purposeful labor of both exegesis and composition revealed in the earliest rabbinic collections. Accordingly, let us turn, for a second exercise of comparison, to an exegetical passage exhibiting clear-cut and fixed forms of rhetoric.

6

Prophecy: Midrash in Matthew's Gospel

We begin with Matthew's Midrash on Isaiah as an exercise in the *Midrash as prophecy*, the reading of the received Scripture in the light of events of history and their meaning for the midrashist. Then we shall reflect upon what we learn from Matthew for our understanding of what Midrash is and how it works.

I present four parallel passages of the First Gospel, in which we find a narrative, culminating in the citation of a verse of Scripture. We have a brief story — such and so happened, was said or was done — followed by a citation of a verse of the Hebrew Scriptures that has been fulfilled in the preceding saying or story. In each case, the purpose of the narrative is not only fulfilled in itself, but also in an explicit subscription linking the narrative to the cited verse and stating explicitly that the antecedent narrative serves to fulfill the prediction contained in the citation from Scripture, hence a convention of theological substance. We deal with Matt. 1:18–23; 2:1–6; 2:16–18; and 3:1–3, all of which conform to this single convention — a boldly original exegetical process.

Now the birth of Jesus Christ took place in this way. When his mother Mary had been betrothed to Joseph, before they came together she was found to be with child of the Holy Spirit; and her husband Joseph, being a just man and unwilling to put her to shame, resolved to divorce her quietly. But as he considered this, behold, an angel of the Lord appeared to him in a dream, saying, "Joseph, son of David, do not fear to take Mary your wife, for that which is conceived in her is of the Holy Spirit; she will bear a son, and you shall call his name Jesus, for he will save his people from their sins." *All this took place to fulfill what the Lord had spoken by the prophet: "Behold, a virgin shall conceive and bear a son, and his name shall be called Emmanuel" (which means, God with us).* (Matt. 1:18–23, italics added)

Now when Jesus was born in Bethlehem of Judea in the days of Herod the king, behold, wise men from the East came to Jerusalem, saying, "Where is he who has been born king of the Jews? For we have seen his star in the East, and have come to worship him." When Herod the king heard this, he was troubled, and all Jerusalem with him; and assembling all the chief priests and scribes of the people, he inquired of them where the Christ was to be born. They told him, "In Bethlehem of Judea; *for so it is written by the prophet: 'And you, O Bethlehem, in the land of Judah, are by no means least among the rulers of Judah; for from you shall come a ruler who will govern my people Israel.'"* (Matt. 2:1–6, italics added)

Then Herod, when he saw that he had been tricked by the wise men, was in a furious rage, and he sent and killed all the male children in Bethlehem and in all that region who were two years old or under, according to the time which he had ascertained from the wise men. *Then was fulfilled what was spoken by the prophet Jeremiah: "A voice was heard in Ramah, wailing and loud lamentation, Rachel weeping for her children; she refused to be consoled, because they were no more."* (Matt. 2:16–18, italics added)

In those days came John the Baptist, preaching in the wilderness of Judea, "Repent, for the kingdom of heaven is at hand." *For this is he who was spoken of by the prophet Isaiah when he said, "The voice of one crying in the wilderness: Prepare the way of the Lord, make his paths straight."* (Matt. 3:1–3, italics added)

The biography of the person under discussion serves as the architectonic principle of the compilation of exegeses into a single statement of meaning. This way of linking exegeses — creating a large-scale collection, as in the earliest rabbinic compilations — shows us another way than the one taken at Qumran, on the one hand, and among the late fourth- and fifth-century compilers of rabbinic collections of exegeses, on the other. What holds the compilation together is the gospel of Jesus Christ; that forms the centerpiece and the principle of cogency. No rabbinic composition in antiquity presents the life of an individual person as the principle of editorial cogency, whether of scriptural exegeses or legal teachings, and the uniqueness of Christianity in its Judaic context is seen in these simple compositions of a highly formalized character in Matthew's Gospel. Elsewhere[1] I have shown that a few stories about the life of Hillel were linked to a sequential set of verses of Deut. 15:1ff. Perhaps someone may have thought of linking events of Hillel's life to a contiguous group of verses. But no "life" of a sage of antiquity forms the base line for a composition, whether made of exegeses, or, more likely, of legal opinions. There are few chapters in the Mishnah, for instance, *m. Kelim* 24, that systematically express the generative principle of a single authority; there are many units of discourse framed around opin-

---

1. Jacob Neusner, "From Exegesis to Fable in Rabbinic Traditions about the Pharisees," *Journal of Jewish Studies* 25 (1974):263.

ions of a single authority, and a great many around disagreements between two or more fixed names. But these are not comparable.

The passages of Matthew, therefore, indicate a clear-cut, distinctive choice on how to compose a "unit of discourse" and to join several congruent units of discourse into a sustained statement—a document. The choice is dictated by the character and purpose of the composition at hand. Since the life of a particular person—as distinct from events of a particular character—forms the focus of discourse, telling a story connected with that life and following this with a citation of the biblical verse illustrated in the foregoing story constitutes the generative and organizing principle of the several units of discourse, all of them within a single taxon. The taxon is not only one-dimensional. It is also rather simple in both its literary traits and its organizing principle. We discern extremely tight narration of a tale, followed by a citation of a verse of Scripture, interpreted only through the device of the explicit joining language: This (1) is what that (2) means. What we see so clearly in the work of the school of Matthew is a simple fact. The work of collating exegeses of Scripture, selecting the appropriate ones and saying important things about them, and the labor of collecting and compiling these exegeses of Scripture into a larger composite together express a single principle, make a single statement, and carry out the purposes of a single polemic.

Three things go together: (1) the principles or processes of exegesis, (2) the purposes of exegesis accomplished in a given interpretation of a single verse, and (3) the formal program of collecting and arranging exegeses into compilations.

The three dimensions of Midrash are thus realized in the prophetic Midrash at hand. In part 3 we shall see how these same three dimensions help us take the measure of the allegorical approach that characterizes the rabbinic sector of Midrash-interpretation of Scripture.

Thus we see, first, that what people said and how they said it go together. What Matthew has taught us is to discern the relationship between form and meaning. He has furthermore shown us how Midrash functions as a work of prophecy. Specifically, Midrash involves *the reading of the verses of ancient Israel's Scriptures in light of their meaning in the life and teachings of Jesus.* What is of special interest here is how the Midrash-exegesis of the cited verses comes to full and rich expression in the Midrash-document, in our case, passages of the Gospel, and, furthermore, fully realizes the Midrash-process that guides the exegete's work. Thus we see the three dimensions of Midrash as prophecy in the Gospels.

What we have in all of the New Testament Gospels, as in the Essene library of Qumran, is an entirely distinctive sort of exegesis: a reading of the verses of ancient Scripture in light of an available scheme of concrete events. The exegete relates Scripture from the past to things that have happened in his own day. His form serves that goal. That is so both for the Essene Midrash and for the Christian Midrash in Matthew. What we learn, which will guide our reading of the Midrash of the rabbinical sages of the dual Torah, is two things: first, that while the exegesis yields results particular to the purpose of its authorship, the basic process of Midrash is uniform; second, that the three dimensions of Midrash form a cogent whole. If in what follows, therefore, the generative principle of exegesis seems alien, the criterion of composition as a whole is entirely familiar. The compiler or evangelist wished to present amplifications of the meaning of a verse of Scripture, not word-for-word or phrase-for-phrase interpretations. He also has not constructed a wide-ranging discussion of the theme of the verse such as we noted in the more philosophical taxon, let alone a mere anthology.

Obviously, there were diverse ways both of undertaking scriptural exegesis and of organizing the collections of such exegeses. In the setting of examples of these other ways in which earlier Jews had responded to verses of Scripture and then collected and organized their responses, obviously there was also more than a single compelling way in which to do the work. It follows that the way in which the framers of *Genesis Rabbah* and *Leviticus Rabbah* did the work was not predictable. Their mode of formulation, organization, and composition therefore is not to be taken for granted. It represented a distinctive choice among possibilities others in Israelite culture had explored.

PART THREE

WHEN THINGS ARE NOT
WHAT THEY SEEM

7

Midrash in the Canon of
the Judaism of the
Dual Torah

Between the first and the seventh centuries, a Judaism took shape around the conviction that at Sinai God revealed to Moses the Torah, or revelation, not only in writing but also orally. This oral Torah was formulated and transmitted in memory, and it was handed on from prophets to sages, from masters to disciples, down from Sinai until it was written down in the Mishnah and successor documents. The Mishnah, a philosophical law code produced at about 200 c.e. out of materials of the preceding two centuries, generated considerable commentary which reached written form in two Talmuds, one in the Land of Israel, the other in Babylonia. Alongside, there was an effort to reread Scripture, that is, the written Torah, and the result was Midrash-compilations. The first of these were given in the names of authorities who appear also in the Mishnah. Since the technical term applied to these authorities was "Tanna," meaning "repeater," that is, one who memorizes and repeats the oral traditions of Sinai, these earlier Midrash-compilations are called "Tannaitic Midrashim." They comprise *Sifra*, for Leviticus, *Sifré*, to Numbers, and another *Sifré*, to Deuteronomy. In general they date to about 300, though that is only a guess. A second set of Midrash-compilations came into existence in the fifth century (ca. 400–450 c.e.): *Genesis Rabbah* and *Leviticus Rabbah*. Still other such compilations were worked out afterward. The Talmud of Babylonia, which comes at the end of the line, in ca. 600, encompassed exegesis of both the Mishnah and Scripture, comprising approximately 60 percent of Mishnah-exegesis and 40 percent of Scripture-exegesis or Midrash for the tractates I have surveyed. When we speak of the Midrash in the canon of the Judaism of the dual Torah, we refer to the Midrash-compilations produced from ca. 200 to 600 among the sages,

43

or rabbis, who preserved and handed on the oral as well as the written Torah of Sinai—so Judaism maintains.

Midrash, as produced by the Judaism of the dual Torah, appeals to some other set of values or considerations than those contained within the verse or topic at hand. Therefore I classify rabbinic Midrash as allegorical, in the sense that it compares something to something else, as does a parable. Some may fairly maintain that Midrash in the Judaism of the dual Torah explains something in terms of something else, as does allegory. Rabbinic Midrash reads Scripture within the principle that things never are what they seem. At the foundations of the hermeneutical pretense lies the long-standing biblical-Jewish insistence that Israel's sorry condition in no way testifies to Israel's true worth—the grandest pretense of all.

The method of rabbinic Midrash therefore involves seeing things as other than they seem. That attitude of mind derives from the mode of thought of Pharisaism. One doctrine of Pharisaism—revealed in its interest in purity laws for the home, not solely for the Temple—required the ordinary Israelite, not of the priestly cult, to pretend to be a priest and therefore keep the cultic rules that apply to the priests' meals at the altar of the Lord. Rabbinic Midrash takes up this same method of pretending that things are other than what they seem to be. The hermeneutic of the dual Torah thus began with the notion that things do not have to be what they seem: the nation now is like the cult then, the ordinary Israelite now like the priest then. The holy way of life lived now, through acts to which merit accrues, corresponds to the holy rites then. The process of metamorphosis is full, rich, complete.

We turn first to the "out-there" of the world to which sages (i.e., rabbis) addressed themselves. Then we shall turn to the "in-here" of how this Midrash-process did its work. When we ask ourselves why rabbinic exegetes appealed to a reality within or beyond the everyday affairs of the workaday world, the answer presents itself with no ambiguity. Israel, God's first love, had suffered the destruction of its holy Temple in 70, and the scriptural prophetic promises of the redemption of Israel were yet to be kept—from a Jewish point of view. Christians, for their part, maintained that those promises had been fulfilled in the return to Zion after the first destruction, in 586, and that Israel could look forward to no further salvation—other than in Jesus Christ.

Christianity did not figure in the sages' system in the first three centuries C.E. But when the Roman emperor converted to Christianity (fourth century) and as Christianity became the religion of the state, the competing faith could no longer be ignored. Christians pointed to the political revolution effected by Constantine as evidence of Christ's kingship. Then, in 360, the last pagan emperor's project of rebuilding Israel's Temple in Jerusalem failed. From that event Christians found still further proof from history and politics for the Jews' error in rejecting Jesus as the Christ. Under such conditions, Scripture would itself serve to confirm the Christians' interpretation of history and politics. From the sages' viewpoint, the crisis of the fourth century found its final solution in the established approach to Scripture: "things are not what they seem."

What changed the sages' world between the advent of the Mishnah in 200 and the making of the major Midrash-compilations at the end of the fourth century, therefore, was the challenge of Christianity. The Mishnah represents the sages' statement prior to that challenge. The Midrash-compilations provide us with their statement after, and in response to, that same challenge. The Mishnah's Judaism did not find necessary a doctrine of the authority of Scripture. There was, moreover, little systematic exegetical effort in the Mishnah at showing the links between the Mishnah and Scripture, that is, within the oral and the written forms of the Torah. The system of the Mishnah, developing a system of Judaism for a world in which Christianity played no considerable role, moreover presented no important doctrine of history and the end of time, stressing the topics of sanctification and neglecting those of salvation. That Judaism therefore took slight interest in the Messiah and presented a teleology (goal of the system) lacking an eschatological and messianic focus. It laid no considerable stress on the symbol of the Torah, though, of course, the Torah as a scroll, as a matter of status, and as revelation of God's will at Sinai, enjoyed prominence. And that Judaism appealed to a document, the Mishnah. The Mishnah was so independent of Scripture that, when the authors wished to say what Scripture had said, they chose to do so in their own words and in their own way. Whatever their intent, it clearly did not encompass explaining to a competing Israel, heirs of the same Scriptures of Sinai, just what authority validated the document, and how the document related to Scripture.

An analysis of the character of the Mishnah is now in order. We take up, first, the negatives, and then return to the powerful and positive effect of the triumph of Christianity in the fourth century upon the sages' Judaism. When we listen to the silences of the Mishnah, as much as to its points of stress, we hear a single message. It is a message of a Judaism that answered a single encompassing question: what, in the aftermath of the destruction of the holy place and holy cult, remained of the sanctity of the holy caste, the priesthood, the holy land, and, above all, the holy people and its holy way of life? The answer would endure: sanctity persists, indelibly, in Israel the people, in its way of life, in its land, in its priesthood, in its food, in its mode of sustaining life, in its manner of procreating and so sustaining the nation. But that answer eventually found itself absorbed within a successor system, with its own points of stress and emphasis. Having now seen where Christianity made no difference, we shall notice when Christianity made all the difference in the world.

There were three specific challenges from Christianity: (1) the claim that Jesus of Nazareth was the Messiah, with the concomitant doctrines of history and salvation on the one side, and symbol of the cross on the other; (2) the church's claim to be the successor of Israel as God's people; and (3) the appeal to Scripture to demonstrate these two propositions. In the formation of the Judaism of the dual Torah, sages produced answers that, for Israel the Jewish people, remained self-evidently valid and compelling so long as the Christian challenge remained vital, well into the nineteenth century. Specifically, sages set forth a doctrine of history and salvation for Israel: Torah encompasses their own Mishnah and related writings as oral part of the one whole Torah revealed by God to Moses at Sinai and a systematic rereading of Scripture to validate through Midrash-compilations made up of Midrash-exegesis of Scripture.

The Midrash produced by the Judaism of the dual Torah addressed the urgent questions raised by Christianity as it assumed control of the Roman Empire. Such Midrash provided self-evidently valid answers for a system deriving its power from the Torah, read by sages, embodied by sages, exemplified by sages, as the reply to Christianity. In this enormous intellectual enterprise we confront the counterpart to the evangelists' rereading of Scripture so as to answer the urgent question (concerning Jesus' identity) facing first-century Christians: Who is it that people say I am? In both cases an extraordinary experience, the one in the encounter with a man beyond time, the other in the meeting of an age beyond all expectation, required the rereading of Scripture in the light of what — in each circumstance — people grasped as the ultimate issue of eternity.

The advent of Midrash-compilations in the Judaism of the dual Torah requires explanation. But the problem is not why Jews in general began to undertake exegeses of the Hebrew Scriptures. No question could be less apt. As we now know, for various groups of Jews Midrash-exegesis was a perfectly routine activity even before the closure and canonization of the Hebrew Scriptures of ancient Israel. Many other kinds of Jews had done so, certainly throughout the preceding thousand years, back to the sixth century B.C.E. Since the Hebrew Bible itself is rich in exegetical materials, with the Books of Chronicles constituting a systematic commentary and revision of the Books of Kings, for example, we cannot ask why at just this time people read and interpreted Scriptures. Judaism in all forms had always done that. The preceding chapters in this book leave no doubt on that score. Nor was there anything new even in collecting exegeses and framing them for a particular polemical purpose, that is, creating a book out of comments on the Scripture and in the form of a commentary. The Essene library at Qumran presents us with compositions of biblical commentary and exegesis. The school of Matthew provides an ample picture of another sort of exercise in systematic composition based on the amplification and application of Israel's ancient Scriptures. We recognize, moreover, that both Israelite communities — the Essenes and the Christian Jews around Matthew — produced their collections not merely to preserve opinions, but to make important statements in a stunning way. We also know, surely in the instance of Matthew, that the power of a brilliantly composed exegetical collection and arrangement can make its impact even after two thousand years. People clearly made and preserved such collections and arrangements to say what they believed God had told them. What was not new, either for the Judaism of the dual Torah or for any other Judaism of the age, was Scripture-exegesis or Midrash. That was a perfectly routine theological venture, which all Judaisms undertook. And every Judaism yielded its Midrash-compilations, as in the case of the Dead Sea Scroll's Judaism and that of Matthew. But for the Judaism of the dual Torah, by contrast, making books out of exegeses of Scripture represented an innovation. The Mishnah, and the exegetical literature that served the Mishnah, did not take shape around the explanation of verses of Scripture. The Mishnah's tractates are organized by topics, and each topic is spelled out in its own terms. But the Midrash-compilations did not work that way. Rather, they would cite and then explain a verse of Scripture, for example, from the Book of Genesis or of Leviticus. And that innovation within the Judaism at hand — represented by the documents of the late third century on the one side, and the early fifth on the other — is what demands our attention.

Why then? Why do it at all? The issue of Midrash-compilations was to show how Scripture was to be read in Israel. That issue became urgent when Christianity made its mark upon sages' consciousness. Then a response was the priority. With Christianity addressing the world (including the Jews) with a systematic exegetical apologetic, beginning of course with Matthew's and the other Gospels' demonstration of how events in the life of Jesus fulfilled prophecy, sages faced the issue of supplying a Judaic response. Their answer took the form of a counter-exegesis. They had not had to do so earlier, because, for the period of the Mishnah, there was no competing group with its alternative reading of Scripture. Now sages confronted a new challenge and they met it.

By the fourth century the church had reached a consensus on the content of the New Testament canon, having earlier accepted as its own the Old Testament (i.e., the Hebrew Bible). Accordingly, the issue of Scripture had come to the fore, and in framing the question of Scripture, the church focused sages' attention on that larger matter of systematic exegesis. When, for example, Jerome referred to the Jews' having a "second" Torah, one that was not authoritative, and when a sequence of important fathers of the church produced exegeses — in profoundly christological terms — of Scripture, the issue was raised. Therefore the sages proceeded to explain the standing of that "second Torah" by producing not merely counter-exegeses to those of the Christians but counter-compilations of such exegeses. To these Midrash-compilations we now turn. Our interest is both literary and theological. We therefore take up three Midrash-compilations and examine their traits and doctrines, and then address three theological issues and see how, in the Midrash-processes of sages, they are worked out.

Now to the "in-here," the specifics of Midrash as a process and hermeneutic. Through Midrash, the rabbinic sages mediated between Israel's perceived condition in an uncertain world and Israel's vivid faith in the God who chooses Israel and reveals the Torah. Faced with an unredeemed world, sages read Scripture as an account of how things are meant to be. To them, things are not what they seem, and that was a judgment made not only about this world but also about Scripture. This world does not testify to God's wish and plan, and Scripture does not record merely the stories and sayings that we read there. This world serves as a metaphor for Scripture's reality, and Scripture provides a metaphor for Israel's as well. Reading one thing in terms of something else, the rabbinic exegetes produced in Midrash a powerful instrument of theological renewal through Scripture.

The verses of Scripture that are quoted in rabbinic Midrash ordinarily shift from the meanings they convey to the implications they contain, so speaking about something, anything, other than what they seem to be saying. The as-if frame of mind brought to Scripture renews Scripture, with the sage seeing everything with fresh eyes. And the result of the new vision was a reimagining of the social world in a given document — the everyday world of Israel in its land in that difficult time. For what the sages now proposed was a reconstruction of existence along the lines of the ancient design of Scripture as they read it: everything that had happened was turned into a repetition of known and already experienced paradigms derived from Scripture, of course — Scripture reread, renewed, reconstructed — along with the society that revered Scripture.

Reading one thing in terms of something else, the builders of the document systematically adopted for themselves the reality of the Scripture, its history and doctrines. They transformed that history from a sequence of one-time events, leading from one place to some other, into an ever-present mythic world. No longer was there one Moses, one David, one set of happenings of a distinctive and never-to-be-repeated character. Now whatever happened of which the thinkers propose to take account must enter and be absorbed into that established and ubiquitous pattern and structure founded in Scripture. It is not that biblical history repeats itself. Rather, biblical history no longer constitutes history as a story of things that happened once, long ago, and pointed to some one moment in the future. Rather, biblical history becomes an account of things that happened every day — hence, an ever-present mythic world. That is why, in Midrash in the Judaism of the dual Torah, Scripture as a whole does not dictate the order of discourse, let alone its character. In this document they chose a verse here, a phrase there. In the more mature Midrash-compilations, such as Leviticus Rabbah and Pesiqta de Rab Kahana, the pretext for propositional discourse is usually out of phase with the cited Scripture passage.

The framers of the Midrash-documents saw Scripture in a new way, just as they saw their own circumstance afresh. That is why they did not write history, an account of what was happening and what it meant. It was not that they did not recognize or appreciate important changes and trends reshaping their nation's life. They could not deny that reality. In their apocalyptic reading of the dietary and leprosy laws (cf. Leviticus Rabbah), they made explicit their close encounter with the history of the world as they knew it. But they had another way of responding to history. It was to treat history as if it were already known and readily understood. Whatever happened had already happened. Scripture dictated the contents of history, laying forth the structures of time, the rules that prevailed and were made known in events. Self-evidently, these same thinkers, projected into Scripture's day the realities of their own, turning Moses and David into rabbis, for example. But that is how people think in that mythic, enchanted world in which reality blends with dream, and hope projects onto future and past alike how people want things to be.

From these somewhat abstract observations we finally come to a concrete account of what happened when the thinkers at hand undertook to reimagine reality — both their own and Scripture's. We briefly state the fundamental message of Essene Midrash and of Christian Midrash as Matthew represents it. Here too, we may represent the recurrent message of rabbinic Midrash in a single paragraph. Deriving from *Leviticus Rabbah*, the message resonates throughout the Midrash-compilations. I summarize in my own words their basic message:

God loves Israel, so gave them the Torah, which defines their life and governs their welfare. Israel is alone in its category (sui generis), so what is a virtue to Israel is a vice to the nation, life-giving to Israel, poison to the Gentiles. True, Israel sins, but God forgives that sin, having punished the nation on account of it. Such a process has yet to come to an end, but it will culminate in Israel's complete regeneration. Meanwhile, Israel's assurance of God's love lies in the many expressions of special concern, for even the humblest and most ordinary aspects of the national life: the food the nation eats, the sexual practices by which it procreates. These life-sustaining, life-transmitting activities draw God's special interest, as a mark of God's general love for Israel. Israel then is supposed to achieve its life in conformity with the marks of God's love. These indications moreover signify also the character of Israel's difficulty, namely, subordination to the nations in general, but to the fourth kingdom, Rome, in particular. Both food laws and skin diseases stand for the nations. There is yet another category of sin, also collective and generative of collective punishment, and that is social. The moral character of Israel's life, the treatment of people by one another, the practice of gossip and small-scale thuggery — these too draw down divine penalty. The nation's fate therefore corresponds to its moral condition. The moral condition, however, emerges not only from the current generation. Israel's richest hope lies in the merit of the ancestors, thus in the scriptural record of the merits attained by the founders of the nation, those who originally brought it into being and gave it life.

When, therefore, sages turned to historical events, reading them as other than what they seemed as they looked upon the world of their day, they quite naturally appealed to Scripture's account of ancient Israel as the model and paradigm for all of history. The one-time events of the generation of the flood, Sodom and Gomorrah, the patriarchs and the sojourn in Egypt, the exodus, the revelation of the Torah at Sinai, the golden calf, the Davidic monarchy and the building of the Temple, Sennacherib, Hezekiah, and the destruction of northern Israel, Nebuchadnezzar and the destruction of the Temple in 586, the life of Israel in Babylonian captivity, Daniel and his associates, Mordecai and

Haman—these events occur over and over again in Midrash-compilations. They turn out to serve as paradigms of sin and atonement, steadfastness and divine intervention, and equivalent lessons. We find, in fact, a fairly standard repertoire of scriptural heroes or villains on the one side, and conventional lists of Israel's enemies and their actions and downfall on the other. The boastful, for instance, include the generation of the flood, Sodom and Gomorrah, Pharaoh, Sisera, Sennacherib, Nebuchadnezzar, the wicked empire (Rome)—contrasted to Israel, "despised and humble in this world." The four kingdoms recur again and again, always ending, of course, with Rome, with the repeated message that after Rome will come Israel. But Israel has to make this happen through its faith and submission to God's will. Lists of enemies repeatedly refer to Cain, the Sodomites, Pharaoh, Sennacherib, Nebuchadnezzar, Haman. These lists of historical figures and events through the power of repetition make a single enormous point. They prove a social law of history.

The catalogues of exemplary villains or heroes and historical events serve a further purpose. They provide a model of how contemporary events are to be absorbed into the biblical paradigm. Since biblical events exemplify recurrent happenings, sin and redemption, forgiveness and atonement, they lose their one-time character. At the same time and in the same way, current events find a place within the ancient, but eternally present, paradigmatic scheme. So no new historical events, other than exemplary episodes in lives of heroes, demand narration because, through what is said about the past, what was happening in the times of the framers of Midrash in the Judaism of the dual Torah would also come under consideration. This mode of dealing with biblical history and contemporary events produces two reciprocal effects: The first is to remove biblical stories from a one-time setting and turn them into accounts of things that happen all the time. The second is that contemporary events—in the fourth or fifth century, for example—lose all of their specificity. Happenings in today's world also enter the paradigmatic framework of established mythic existence. So (1) the Scripture's myth happens every day, and (2) every day produces reenactment of the Scripture's myth. What that means in the actual encounter with Scripture we shall now examine.

8

Midrash and Genesis

In the Book of Genesis, as the sages or rabbis who composed *Genesis Rabbah* (ca. 400–450) read Scripture's account of creation and the beginnings of Israel, God set forth to Moses the entire scope and meaning of Israel's history among the nations and salvation at the end of days. Genesis drew their attention more than any other book of the Pentateuch—the five books of Moses. Sages read Genesis not as a set of individual verses, one by one, but as a single and coherent statement, whole and complete. Let me restate in my own words the conviction of the framers of *Genesis Rabbah* about the message and meaning of the Book of Genesis:

We now know what will be in the future. Just as Jacob had told his sons what would happen in time to come, just as Moses told the tribes their future, so we may understand the laws of history if we study the Torah. And in the Torah we turn to beginnings: the rules as they were laid out at the very start of human history. These we find in the Book of Genesis, the story of the origins of the world and of Israel.

The Torah tells us not only what happened but why. The Torah permits us to discover the laws of history. Once we know those laws, we may also peer into the future and come to an assessment of what is going to happen to us—and, especially, of how we shall be saved from our present existence. Because everything exists under the aspect of a timeless will, God's will, and all things express one thing, God's program and plan, in the Torah we uncover the workings of God's will. Our task as Israel is to accept, endure, submit, and celebrate. So our sages found lessons not only for the future but also for today: hope not despair, courage not cowardice, belief and faith and trust in God in difficult times.

This is a fine example of how sages read Scripture: things were not what they seemed to be but meant something else altogether. In general people read the Book of Genesis as the story of how Israel saw the past, not the future: the beginning of the world and of Israel, humanity from

Adam to Noah, then from Noah to Abraham, and the story of the three patriarchs and four matriarchs of Israel (Abraham, Isaac, Jacob, Sarah, Rebecca, Leah, and Rachel), and, finally, Joseph and his brothers — from creation to the descent into Egypt. But to the rabbis who created *Genesis Rabbah*, the Book of Genesis tells the story of Israel, the Jewish people, in the here and now. The principle was that what happened to the patriarchs and matriarchs signals what will happen to their descendants: the model of the ancestors sends a message for the children. So the importance of Genesis, as the sages of *Genesis Rabbah* read the book, derives not from its lessons about the past but its message for Israel's present — and, especially, future.

Their conviction is that what Abraham, Isaac, and Jacob did shaped the future history of Israel. But the interest of rabbinic Midrash is not merely in history as a source of lessons but as the treasury of truths about the here and now and especially about tomorrow. What the patriarchs did supplies the model, the message, the meaning for what we should do. To sages the world reveals not chaos but order, and God's will works itself out not once but again and again. If, they held, we can find out how things got going, then we also can find meaning in today and method in where we are heading.

A concrete example from rabbinic Midrash is now in order. To see what they did, we turn to their doctrine of Rome. Recall that Christian Rome's claim to be Israel precipitated a crisis. The sages of *Genesis Rabbah* dealt with this crisis by conceding that Christian Rome required attention in a way in which pagan Rome had not. Furthermore, they appealed to their established theory of who Israel is in order to find a place for Rome. They saw Israel as one big family, children of Abraham, Isaac, Jacob. In order to fit Rome into this system, they had to make room for Rome in the family. Scripture speaks of deeper truths. Hence when Scripture tells the story of certain members of the family, "we" who understand Scripture know that what is meant is a member whom only now we recognize. Specifically, Rome now is represented by Esau then (Jacob's brother, Jacob's enemy). Or Rome may be Ishmael or Moab. "And we? We are Israel." Scripture therefore tells the story of Esau and Jacob, who are, in today's world, Rome and Israel. And Jacob supplants Esau. Jacob wins the blessing and the patrimony and the birthright. Jacob will again, that is, Israel even now will succeed (Esau=Rome). Things are not what they seem, Scripture speaks of other things than those on the surface, and Midrash-exegesis tells that story.

That is an example of reading one thing in light of something else, and everything as though it meant something other than what it said.

Identifying Rome as Esau is a fresh idea. In the Mishnah, two hundred years earlier, Rome appears as a place, not as a symbol. But in *Genesis Rabbah* Rome is symbolized by Esau. But why Esau? Because Esau is a sibling: relation, competitor, enemy, brother. In choosing Rome as the counterpart to Israel, sages simply opened Genesis and found there Israel (Jacob) and his brother, his enemy—Esau. Why not understand the obvious: Esau stands for Rome, Jacob for Israel, and their relationship represents then what Israel and Rome would work out even now, in the fourth century, the first century of Christian rule. Esau rules now, but Jacob possesses the birthright. Esau/Rome personifies the last of the four great empires (Persia, Media, Greece, Rome). On the other side of Rome? Israel's age of glory. And why is Rome now brother? Because, after all, the Christians do claim a common patrimony in Hebrew Scriptures and do claim to be a part of Israel. That claim was not ignored, it was answered by the exegetes: yes, part of Israel, the rejected part. Jacob bears the blessing and transmits the blessing to humanity, Esau does not.

That concession—Rome is a sibling, a close relative of Israel—represents an implicit recognition of Christianity's claim to share the patrimony of Judaism, to be descended from Abraham and Isaac. So how are we to deal with the glory and the power of our brother, Esau? And what are we to say about the claim of Esau to enthrone Christ? And how are we to assess today the future history of Israel, the salvation of God's first, best love? It is not by denying Rome's claim but by evaluating it, not by turning a back to the critical events of the hour but by confronting those events authoritatively. In this instance we see how rabbinic Midrash resorted to an allegorical or parabolic reading of Scripture to bring to Scripture the issues of the age and to discover God's judgment of those issues. We now turn to a detailed examination of how sages spelled out what Scripture really means. To sages Genesis reported what really happened. But Genesis also spelled out the meanings and truth of what they saw happen. In the following passage we have Esau in place of Rome:[1]

Genesis Rabbah LXI:VII

2

A. "[*But to the sons of his concubines, Abraham gave gifts, and while he was still living,*] *he sent them away from his son Isaac, eastward to the east country*" (Gen. 25:6):

B. He said to them, "Go as far to the east as you can, so as not to be burned by the flaming coal of Isaac."

1. All translations in this chapter are by the author.

C. But because Esau came to make war with Jacob, he took his appropriate share on his account: *"Is this your joyous city, whose feet in antiquity, in ancient days, carried her afar off to sojourn? Who has devised this against Tyre, the crowning city?"* (Isa. 23:7).

D. Said R. Eleazar, "Whenever the name of Tyre is written in Scripture, if it is written out [with all of the letters], then it refers to the province of Tyre. Where it is written without all of its letters [and so appears identical to the word of enemy], the reference of Scripture is to Rome. [So the sense of the verse is that Rome will receive its appropriate reward.]"

Number 2 carries forward the eschatological reading of the incident of Gen. 25:6. Israel's later history is prefigured in the gift to Isaac and the rejection of the other sons. The self-evidence that Esau's reward will be recompense for his evil indicates that the passage draws upon sarcasm to make its point. Sages essentially looked to the facts of history for the laws of history. We may compare them to social scientists or social philosophers, trying to turn anecdotes into insight and to demonstrate how we may know the difference between impressions and truths. Genesis provided facts. Careful sifting of those facts will yield the laws that dictated why things happened one way rather than some other. The language, as much as the substance, of the narrative provided facts demanding careful study. We understand why sages thought so, if we call to mind their basic understanding of the Torah. To them (as to many today, myself included) the Torah came from God and in every detail contained revelation of God's truth. Accordingly, just as we study nature and derive facts demanding explanation and yielding law, so we study Scripture and find facts susceptible of explanation and yielding truth.

Consider an exemplary case of how sages discovered social laws of history in the facts of Scripture. What Abraham did corresponds to what Balaam did, and the same law of social history derives proof from each of the two contrasting figures.

Genesis Rabbah LV:VIII

1

A. *"And Abraham rose early in the morning, [saddled his ass, and took two of his young men with him, and his son Isaac, and he cut the wood for the burnt offering and arose and went to the place which God had told him]"* (Gen. 22:3):

B. Said R. Simeon b. Yohai, "Love disrupts the natural order of things, and hatred disrupts the natural order of things.

C. "Love disrupts the natural order of things we learn from the case of Abraham: ' . . . *he saddled his ass.*' But did he not have any number of servants? But that proves love disrupts the natural order of things.

D. "Hatred disrupts the natural order of things we learn from the case of Balaam: *'And Balaam rose up early in the morning and saddled his ass'* (Num.

22:21). But did he not have any number of servants? But that proves hatred disrupts the natural order of things.

E. "Love disrupts the natural order of things we learn from the case of Joseph: *'And Joseph made his chariot ready'* (Gen. 46:29). But did he not have any number of servants? But that proves love disrupts the natural order of things.

F. "Hatred disrupts the natural order of things we learn from the case of Pharaoh: *'And he made his chariot ready'* (Exod. 14:6). But did he not have any number of servants? But that proves hatred disrupts the natural order of things."

The social law about the overriding effect of love or hatred is disclosed by diverse cases. Now we move from the laws of social history to the rules that govern Israel's history in particular.

2

A. Said R. Simeon b. Yohai, "Let one act of saddling an ass come and counteract another act of saddling the ass. May the act of saddling the ass done by our father Abraham, so as to go and carry out the will of him who spoke and brought the world into being, counteract the act of saddling that was carried out by Balaam when he went to curse Israel.

B. "Let one act of preparing counteract another act of preparing. Let Joseph's act of preparing his chariot so as to meet his father serve to counteract Pharaoh's act of preparing to go and pursue Israel."

C. R. Ishmael taught on Tannaite authority, "Let the sword held in the hand serve to counteract the sword held in the hand.

D. "Let the sword held in the hand of Abraham, as it is said, *'Then Abraham put forth his hand and took the knife to slay his son'* (Gen. 22:10), serve to counteract the sword taken by Pharaoh in hand: *'I will draw my sword, my hand shall destroy them'* (Exod. 15:9)."

We see that the narrative of Genesis is carefully culled for probative facts, which are meant to be generalized into laws. One fact is that there are laws of history. The other is that laws may be set aside, by either love or hatred. Yet another law of history applies in particular to Israel, as distinct from the foregoing, deriving from the life of both Israel and the nations, Abraham and Balaam.

Here is an exercise in the recurrent proof of a single proposition that Abraham foresaw the future history of Israel, with special reference to the rule of the four monarchies, Babylonia, Media, Greece, then Rome — prior to the rule of Israel:

Genesis Rabbah XLIV:XVII

4

A. "[*And it came to pass, as the sun was going down,*] *lo, a deep sleep fell on Abram, and lo, a dread and great darkness fell upon him*" (Gen. 15:12):

B. ". . . *lo, a dread*" refers to Babylonia, as it is written, "*Then was Nebuchadnezzar filled with fury*" (Gen. 3:19).

C. ". . . *and darkness*" refers to Media, which darkened the eyes of Israel by making it necessary for the Israelites to fast and conduct public mourning.

56

D. ". . . *great* . . ." refers to Greece.

G. ". . . *fell upon him*" refers to Edom [Rome], as it is written, "*The earth quakes at the noise of their fall*" (Jer. 49:21).

I find this a particularly moving tableau, with darkness descending and dread falling on Jacob. That accounts, also, for the power of the ideas at hand. For no. 4 successfully links Gen. 15:12 to the history of Israel. Israel's history falls under God's dominion. Whatever will happen carries out God's plan. The fourth kingdom is part of that plan, which we can discover by carefully studying Abraham's life and God's Word to him. In the following selection, we see an explicit effort to calculate the time at which the end will come and Israel will be saved:

Genesis Rabbah XLIV:XVIII

1

A. "*Then the Lord said to Abram, 'Know of a surety* [*that your descendants will be sojourners in a land that is not theirs, and they will be slaves there, and they will be oppressed for four hundred years; but I will bring judgment on the nation which they serve, and afterward they shall come out with great possessions*]" (Gen. 15:13–14):

B. "*Know*" that I shall scatter them.

C. "*Of a certainty*" that I shall bring them back together again.

D. "*Know*" that I shall put them out as a pledge [in expiation of their sins].

E. "*Of a certainty*" that I shall redeem them.

F. "*Know*" that I shall make them slaves.

G. "*Of a certainty*" that I shall free them.

2

A. ". . . *that your descendants will be sojourners in a land that is not theirs and they will be slaves there, and they will be oppressed for four hundred years*":

B. It is four hundred years from the point at which you will produce a descendant. [The Israelites will not serve as slaves for four hundred years, but that figure refers to the passage of time from Isaac's birth.]

C. Said R. Yudan, "The condition of being outsiders, the servitude, the oppression in a land that was not theirs all together would last for four hundred years, that was the requisite term."

Number 1 analyzes the cited verse and joins within its simple formula the entire history of Israel, punishment and forgiveness alike. Number 2 does the same for the verse to follow, trying to bring it into line with the chronology of Israel's later history.

The single most important paradigm for history emerged from the deed at Moriah, the binding of Isaac on the altar as a sacrifice to God, a critical motif in synagogue art as well, as the philosopher-artists of synagogue decoration also created their Midrash. Here is how sages derive enduring rules of history and salvation from the story of the willingness of Abraham to sacrifice even his son to God:

Genesis Rabbah LVI:I

1

A. *"On the third day Abraham lifted up his eyes and saw the place afar off"* (Gen. 22:4):

B. *"After two days he will revive us, on the third day he will raise us up, that we may live in his presence"* (Hosea 16:2).

C. On the third day of the tribes: *"And Joseph said to them on the third day, 'This do and live' "* (Gen. 42:18).

D. On the third day of the giving of the Torah: *"And it came to pass on the third day when it was morning"* (Exod. 19:16).

E. On the third day of the spies: *"And hide yourselves there for three days"* (Josh. 2:16).

F. On the third day of Jonah: *"And Jonah was in the belly of the fish three days and three nights"* (Jonah 2:1).

G. On the third day of the return from the exile: *"And we abode there three days"* (Ezra 8:32).

H. On the third day of the resurrection of the dead: *"After two days he will revive us, on the third day he will raise us up, that we may live in his presence"* (Hosea 16:2).

I. On the third day of Esther: *"Now it came to pass on the third day that Esther put on her royal apparel"* (Esth. 5:1).

J. She put on the monarchy of the house of her fathers.

K. On account of what sort of merit?

L. Rabbis say, "On account of the third day of the giving of the Torah."

M. R. Levi said, "It is on account of the merit of the third day of Abraham: *'On the third day Abraham lifted up his eyes and saw the place afar off'* (Gen. 22:4)."

The third day marks the fulfillment of the promise, at the end of time, of the resurrection of the dead, and, at appropriate moments, of Israel's redemption. The reference to the third day at Gen. 22:4 then invokes the entire panoply of Israel's history. The relevance of the composition emerges at the end. Prior to the concluding segment, the passage forms a kind of litany and falls into the category of a liturgy. Still, the recurrent hermeneutic which teaches that the stories of the patriarchs prefigure the history of Israel certainly makes its appearance. Our final example makes the point still more explicitly:

Genesis Rabbah LVI:II

4

A. *". . . and we will worship [through an act of prostration] and come again to you"* (Gen. 22:5):

B. He thereby told him that he would come back from Mount Moriah whole and in peace [for he said that *we* shall come back].

5

A. Said R. Isaac, "And all was on account of the merit attained by the act of prostration.

B. "Abraham returned in peace from Mount Moriah only on account of the merit owing to the act of prostration: '. . . and we will worship [through an act of prostration] and come [then, on that account] again to you' (Gen. 22:5).

C. "The Israelites were redeemed only on account of the merit owing to the act of prostration: 'And the people believed . . . then they bowed their heads and prostrated themselves' (Exod. 4:31).

D. "The Torah was given only on account of the merit owing to the act of prostration: 'And worship [prostrate themselves you afar off' (Exod. 24:1).

E. "Hannah was remembered only on account of the merit owing to the act of prostration: 'And they worshiped before the Lord' (1 Sam. 1:19).

F. "The exiles will be brought back only on account of the merit owing to the act of prostration: 'And it shall come to pass in that day that a great horn shall be blown and they shall come that were lost . . . and that were dispersed . . . and they shall worship the Lord in the holy mountain of Jerusalem' (Isa. 27:13).

G. "The Temple was built only on account of the merit owing to the act of prostration: 'Exalt you the Lord our God and worship at his holy hill' (Ps. 99:9).

H. "The dead will live only on account of the merit owing to the act of prostration: 'Come let us worship and bend the knee, let us kneel before the Lord our maker' (Ps. 95:6)."

Number 4 draws a lesson from the use of "thus" in the cited verses. The sizable construction at no. 5 makes a simple point, to which our base verse provides its modest contribution. But its polemic is hardly simple. The entire history of Israel flows from its acts of worship ("prostration") and is unified by a single law. That law is simple: every sort of advantage Israel has ever gained came about through worship. Hence what is besought, in the elegant survey, is the law of history. The Scripture then supplies those facts from which the governing law is derived. The lesson that Israel commands its own destiny through obedience to God emerges in every line of Genesis. In the hands of the sages of *Genesis Rabbah*, the book of the beginnings tells the tale of the end time.

9

Midrash and Leviticus

When things are not what they seem, Midrash as a process of allegory transforms Scripture. When the sages came to Leviticus, they accomplished a remarkable transformation, for they turned a book that focuses upon the perpetual sanctification of Israel in the eternal cult of the Temple into a picture of the one-time events that yield reliable historical laws pointing toward the salvation of Israel at the end of time. The Book of Leviticus, which concerns the sanctification of Israel's priesthood, is thereby turned into a treatise on salvation and Israel's society as a whole. That subject scarcely appears within its pages, and thus Leviticus is changed from one thing into something else.

Precisely how allegory works for sage-exegetes emerges in the following passage, which treats the animals that Israel is forbidden to eat as allegories for the rule of the monarchies, ending of course with Rome as worst but also last, to which Israel is subjugated. What we see in *Leviticus Rabbah* (which came to redaction approximately a generation after *Genesis Rabbah*, in ca. 450 C.E.) is consistent with what we have already observed in *Genesis Rabbah*: sages absorb one-time events into their system of classification of regularities and rules — the opposite of one-time events. Allegory serves as an ideal mode of classification, since it allows many things to be transformed into some few, readily classified, ones.

The passage takes up a proposition, which is then proved through the systematic compilation of lists of facts against which the proposition is tested and through which it is validated. What I explained in chapter 8 about the basic mode of thought of rabbinic Midrash — transforming the detail into an example or a general rule — here finds striking exemplification. We now turn to the relevant passages of *Leviticus Rabbah*[1]

1. All translations in this chapter are by the author.

where we see example after example of the opening proposition, that the prophets foresaw Israel's history, which yields the important syllogism: after Rome comes Israel.

Leviticus Rabbah XIII:V

1

A. Said R. Ishmael b. R. Nebemiah, "All the prophets foresaw what the pagan kingdoms would do [to Israel).

B. "The first man foresaw what the pagan kingdoms would do [to Israel].

C. "That is in line with the following verse of Scripture: 'A river flowed out of Eden [to water the garden, and there it divided and became four rivers]' (Gen. 2:10). [The four rivers stand for the four kingdoms, Babylonia, Media, Greece, and Rome.]"

How each of the rivers of Eden represents one of the four kingdoms, and why that fact bears meaning for Israel's future history, is then spelled out.

3

A. "[There it divided] and became four rivers" (Gen. 2:10) — this refers to the four kingdoms.

B. "The name of the first is Pishon (PSWN); [it is the one which flows around the whole land of Havilah, where there is gold; and the gold of that land is good; bdellium and onyx stone are there]" (Gen. 2:11–12).

C. This refers to Babylonia, on account [of the reference to Babylonia in the following verse:] "And their [the Babylonians'] horsemen spread themselves (PSW)" (Hab. 1:8).

D. [It is further] on account of [Nebuchadnezzar's being] a dwarf, shorter than ordinary men by a handbreadth.

E. "[It is the one which flows around the whole land of Havilah" (Gen. 2:11).

F. "This [reference to the river's flowing around the whole land] speaks of Nebuchadnezzar, the wicked man, who came up and surrounded the entire Land of Israel, which places its hope in the Holy One, blessed be he."

G. That is in line with the following verse of Scripture: "Hope in God, for I shall again praise him" (Ps. 42:5).

4

A. "The name of the second river is Gihon; [it is the one which flows around the whole land of Cush]" (Gen. 2:13).

B. This refers to Media, which produced Haman, that wicked man, who spit out venom like a serpent.

C. It is on account of the verse: "On your belly will you go" (Gen. 3:14).

D. "It is the one which flows around the whole land of Cush" (Gen. 2:13).

E. [We know that this refers to Media, because it is said:] "Who rules from India to Cush" (Esth. 1:1).

5

A. "And the name of the third river is Tigris (HDQL), [which flows east of Assyria]" (Gen. 2:14).

B. This refers to Greece [Syria], which was sharp (HD) and speedy (QL) in making its decrees, saying to Israel, "Write on the horn of an ox that you have no portion in the God of Israel."

C. "Which flows east (QDMT) of Assyria" (Gen. 2:14).

D. Said R. Huna, "In three aspects the kingdom of Greece was in advance (QDMH) of the present evil kingdom [Rome]: in respect to shipbuilding, the arrangement of camp vigils, and language."

E. Said R. Huna, "Any and every kingdom may be called 'Assyria' (ashur), on account of all of their making themselves powerful at Israel's expense."

F. Said R. Yose b. R. Hanina, "Any and every kingdom may be called Nineveh (NNWH), on account of their adorning (NWY) themselves at Israel's expense."

G. Said R. Yose b. R. Hanina, "Any and every kingdom may be called Egypt (MSRYM), on account of their oppressing (MSRYRM) Israel."

6

A. "And the fourth river is the Euphrates (PRT)" (Gen. 2:14).

B. This refers to Edom [Rome], since it was fruitful (PRT), and multiplied through the prayer of the elder [Isaac at Gen. 27:39].

C. Another interpretation: "It was because it was fruitful and multiplied, and so cramped his world."

D. Another explanation: "Because it was fruitful and multiplied and cramped his son."

E. Another explanation: "Because it was fruitful and multiplied and cramped his house."

F. Another explanation: "Parat"—because in the end, "I am going to exact a penalty from it."

G. That is in line with the following verse of Scripture: "I have trodden (PWRH) the winepress alone" (Isa. 63:3).

We now come to a passage that we have already seen. The proof of the proposition that the prophets foresaw the future history of Israel derives from the following *Gen. R.* 42:2: Abraham foresaw what the evil kingdoms would do [to Israel]. We proceed to other prophets.

8

A. Daniel foresaw what the evil kingdoms would do [to Israel].

B. "Daniel said, I saw in my vision by night, and behold, the four winds of heaven were stirring up the great sea. And four great beasts came up out of the sea, [different from one another. The first was like a lion and had eagles' wings. Then as I looked, its wings were plucked off . . . And behold, another beast, a second one, like a bear . . . After this I looked, and lo, another, like a leopard . . . After this I saw in the night visions, and behold, a fourth beast, terrible and dreadful and exceedingly strong; and it has great iron teeth]" (Dan. 7:3–7).

C. If you enjoy sufficient merit, it will emerge from the sea, but if not, it will come out of the forest.

D. The animal that comes up from the sea is not violent, but the one that comes up out of the forest is violent.

E. Along these same lines: "The boar out of the wood ravages it" (Ps. 80:14).

F. If you enjoy sufficient merit, it will come from the river, and if not, from the forest.

G. The animal that comes up from the river is not violent, but the one that comes up out of the forest is violent.

H. *"Different from one another"* (Dan. 7:3).

I. Differing from (hating) one another.

J. This teaches that every nation that rules in the world hates Israel and reduces them to slavery.

K. *"The first was like a lion [and had eagles' wings]"* (Dan. 7:4).

L. This refers to Babylonia.

M. Jeremiah saw [Babylonia] as a lion. Then he went and saw it as an eagle.

N. He saw it as a lion: *"A lion has come up from his thicket"* (Jer. 4:7).

O. And [as an eagle:] *"Behold, he shall come up and swoop down as the eagle"* (Jer. 49:22).

P. People said to Daniel, "What do you see?"

Q. He said to them, "I see the face like that of a lion and wings like those of an eagle: *'The first was like a lion and had eagles' wings. Then, as I looked, its wings were plucked off, and it was lifted up from the ground [and made to stand upon two feet like a man and the heart of a man was given to it]'"* (Dan. 7:4).

R. R. Eleazar and R. Ishmael b. R. Nehemiah:

S. R. Eleazar said. "While the entire lion was smitten, its heart was not smitten.

T. "That is in line with the following statement: *'And the heart of a man was given to it'* (Dan. 7:4)."

U. And R. Ishmael b. R. Nehemiah said, "Even its heart was smitten, for it is written, *'Let his heart be changed from a man's'* (Dan. 4:17).

X. *"And behold, another beast, a second one, like a bear. [It was raised up one side; it had three ribs in its mouth between its teeth, and it was told, Arise, devour much flesh]"* (Dan. 7:5).

Y. This refers to Media.

Z. Said R. Yohanan, "It is like a bear."

AA. It is written, *"similar to a wolf'* (DB); thus, "And a wolf was there."

BB. That is in accord with the view of R. Yohanan, for R. Yohanan said, *"'Therefore a lion out of the forest [slays them]'* (Jer. 5:6) — this refers to Babylonia.

CC. *"'A wolf of the deserts spoils them'* (Jer. 5:6) refers to Media.

DD. *"'A leopard watches over their cities'* (Jer. 5:6) refers to Greece.

EE. *"'Whoever goes out from them will be savaged'* (Jer. 5:6) refers to Edom.

FF. "Why so? *'Because their transgressions are many, and their backslidings still more'* (Jer. 5:6)."

GG. *"After this, I looked, and lo, another, like a leopard [with four wings of a bird on its back; and the beast had four heads; and dominion was given to it]"* (Dan. 7:6).

HH. This [leopard] refers to Greece, which persisted impudently in making harsh decrees, saying to Israel, "Write on the horn of an ox that you have no share in the God of Israel."

II. *"After this I saw in the night visions, and behold, a fourth beast, terrible and dreadful and exceedingly strong; [and it had great iron teeth; it devoured and broke in pieces and stamped the residue with its feet. It was different from all the beasts that were before it; and it had ten horns]"* (Dan. 7:7).

JJ. This refers to Edom [Rome].

KK. Daniel saw the first three visions on one night, and this one he saw on another night. Now why was that the case?

LL. R. Yohanan and R. Simeon b. Laquish:

MM. R. Yohanan said, "It is because the fourth beast weighed as much as the first three."

NN. And R. Simeon b. Laqish said, "It outweighed them."

OO. R. Yohanan objected to R. Simeon b. Laqish, *"Prophesy, therefore, son of man, clap your hands [and let the sword come down twice; yea, thrice. The sword for those to be slain; it is the sword for the great slaughter, which encompasses them]* (Ezek. 21:14-15). [So the single sword of Rome weighs against the three others]."

PP. And R. Simeon b. Laqish, how does he interpret the same passage? He notes that [the threefold sword] is doubled (Ezek. 21:14), [thus outweighs the three swords, equally twice their strength].

Now comes the most powerful allegorization of all: the reading of the animals of Deut. 14:7 — which Israelites may not eat, despite their apparent acceptability — as if they were the four monarchies.

9

A. Moses foresaw what the evil kingdoms would do [to Israel].

B. *"The camel, rock badger, and hare"* (Deut. 14:7). [Compare: *"Nevertheless, among those that chew the cud or part the hoof, you shall not eat these: the camel, because it chews the cud but does not part the hoof, is unclean to you. The rock badger, because it chews the cud but does not part the hoof, is unclean to you. And the hare, because it chews the cud but does not part the hoof, is unclean to you, and the pig, because it parts the hoof and is cloven-footed, but does not chew the cud, is unclean to you"* (Lev. 11:4-8).]

Once more, there are plays on words, in which the letters that stand for an animal are read with vowels that yield a different word altogether, as in the following.

C. *"The camel"* (GML) refers to Babylonia, [in line with the following verse of Scripture: *"O daughter of Babylonia, you who are to be devastated!]* Happy will be he who requites (GML) you, with what you have done to us"* (Ps. 147:8).

D. *"The rock badger"* (Deut. 14:7) — this refers to Media.

E. Rabbis and R. Judah b. R. Simon.

F. Rabbis say, "Just as the rock badger exhibits traits of uncleanness and traits of cleanness, so the kingdom of Media produced both a righteous man and a wicked one."

G. Said R. Judah b. R. Simon, "The last Darius was Esther's son. He was clean on his mother's side and unclean on his father's side."

H. *"The hare"* (Deut. 14:7) — this refers to Greece. The mother of King Ptolemy was named "Hare" [in Greek: *lagos*].

I. *"The pig"* (Deut. 14:7) — this refers to Edom [Rome].

J. Moses made mention of the first three in a single verse and the final one in a verse by itself [Deut. 14:7,8]. Why so?

K. R. Yohanan and R. Simeon b. Laqish.

L. R. Yohanan said, "It is because [the pig] is equivalent to the other three."
[That is, Rome outweighs in evil the other three monarchies put together.]

M. And R. Simeon b. Laqish said, "It is because it outweighs them."

N. R. Yohanan objected to R. Simeon b. Laqish, " 'Prophesy, therefore, son
of man, clap your hands [and let the sword come down twice, yea thrice]'
(Ezek. 21:14)."

O. And how does R. Simeon b. Laqish interpret the same passage? He notes
that [the threefold sword] is doubled (Ezek. 21:14).

What follows is shared with *Genesis Rabbah* and serves as an appendix
to the proposition that all the prophets foresaw Israel's future history.
The appendix now dwells on the point that only two of the prophets
realized how evil Rome would be.

10

A. [*Gen. R.* 65:1:] R. Phineas and R. Hilqiah in the name of R. Simon:
"Among all the prophets, only two of them revealed [the true evil of Rome],
Assaf and Moses.

B. "Assaf said, '*The pig out of the wood ravages it*' (Ps. 80:14).

C. "Moses said, '*And the pig, [because it parts the hoof and is cloven footed
but does not chew the cud]*' (Lev. 11:7).

D. "Why is [Rome] compared to a pig?

E. "It is to teach you the following: Just as, when a pig crouches and produces
its hooves, it is as if to say, 'See how I am clean [since I have a cloven hoof],' so
the evil kingdom takes pride, seizes by violence, and steals, and then gives the
appearance of establishing a tribunal for justice."

The task facing the exegete was to make sense of Rome as Christian.
Sages had to find an appropriate classification for a Rome that was neither pagan nor Israel. To relate any nation to Israel, sages could appeal
only to the operative political metaphor that in their minds explained
who was Israel, that is, genealogy. A place had to be found for Rome
in the family history of Israel, for Christian Rome did, after all, claim
to be part of that history and heir to its blessing. Hence Rome was represented, allegorically, by Ishmael, Esau, or Edom — the rejected side of
the family of Israel. Here we have yet another exercise: Rome pretends
to be Israel but is not, as the pig pretends to be suitable for Israelite con-
sumption but is not.

12

A. Another interpretation [of GRH, "cud," now with reference to GR,
"stranger":]

B. "*The camel*" (Lev. 11:4) — this refers to Babylonia.

C. "*For it chews the cud*" [now: brings up the stranger] — for it exalts righteous men: "*And Daniel was in the gate of the king*" (Dan. 2:49).

D. "*The rock badger*" (Lev. 11:5) — this refers to Media.

E. "*For it brings up the stranger*" — for it exalts righteous men: "*Mordecai sat
at the gate of the king*" (Esth. 2:19).

F. *"The hare"* (Lev. 11:6) — this refers to Greece.

G. *"For it brings up the stranger"*— for it exalts the righteous.

H. When Alexander of Macedonia saw Simeon the Righteous, he would rise up on his feet. They said to him, "Can't you see the Jew, that you stand up before this Jew?"

I. He said to them, "When I go forth to battle, I see something like this man's visage, and I conquer."

J. *"The pig"* (Lev. 11:7) — this refers to Rome.

K. *"But it does not bring up the stranger"*— for it does not exalt the righteous.

L. And it is not enough that it does not exalt them, but it kills them.

M. That is in line with the following verse of Scripture: *"I was angry with my people, I profaned my heritage; I gave them into your hand, you showed them no mercy; on the aged you made your yoke exceedingly heavy"* (Isa. 47:6).

N. This refers to R. Aqiba and his colleagues [who were martyred by Rome].

13

A. Another interpretation [now treating "bring up the cud" (GR) as "bring along in its train" (GRR)]:

What is coming is a direct comment on the sequence of empires, leading to the rise of Israel to rule.

B. *"The camel"* (Lev. 11:4) — this refers to Babylonia.

C. *"Which brings along in its train"*— for it brought along another kingdom after it.

D. *"The rock badger"* (Lev. 11:5) — this refers to Media.

E. *"Which brings along in its train"*— for it brought along another kingdom after it.

F. *"The hare"* (Lev. 11:6) — this refers to Greece.

G. *"Which brings along in its train"*— for it brought along another kingdom after it.

H. *"The pig"* (Lev. 11:7) — this refers to Rome.

I. *"Which does not bring along in its train"*— for it did not bring along another kingdom after it.

J. And why is it then called "pig" (HZYR)? For it restores (MHZRT) the crown to the one who truly should have it [namely, Israel, whose dominion will begin when the rule of Rome ends].

K. That is in line with the following verse of Scripture: *"And saviors will come up on Mount Zion to judge the Mountain of Esau [Rome], and the kingdom will then belong to the Lord"* (Obad. 1:21).

The concluding comment forms the climax and the goal of the whole composition: Israel will rule in the end, after Rome.

To stand back and consider this vast apocalyptic vision of Israel's history, we first review the overall message. This comes in two parts, first the explicit, then the implicit. As to the former, the first claim is that God had told the prophets what would happen to Israel at the hands of the pagan kingdoms, Babylonia, Media, Greece, Rome. These are further represented by Nebuchadnezzar, Haman, Alexander for Greece, Edom or Esau, interchangeably, for Rome. The same vision came from Adam, Abraham, Daniel, and Moses. The same policy toward Israel — oppression, destruction, enslavement, alienation from the true God — emerged from all four.

How does Rome stand out? First, it was made fruitful through the prayer of Isaac in behalf of Esau. Second, Edom is represented by the fourth and final beast. Rome is related through Esau; Babylonia, Media, and Greece are not. The fourth beast was seen in a vision separate from the first three. It was worst of all and outweighed the rest. In the apocalyptic interpretation of the animals of Lev. 11:4–8/Deut. 14:7 (the camel, rock badger, hare, and pig), the pig, standing for Rome, again emerges as different from the others and more threatening than the rest. Just as the pig pretends to be a clean beast by showing the cloven hoof, but in fact is an unclean one, so Rome pretends to be just but in fact governs by thuggery. Edom does not pretend to praise God but only blasphemes. It does not exalt the righteous but kills them. These symbols concede nothing to Christian monotheism and biblicism. Of greatest importance — while all the other beasts bring further ones in their wake, the pig does not: "It does not bring another kingdom after it." It will restore the crown to the one who will truly deserve it, Israel. Esau will be judged by Zion, so Obad. 1:21.

Now how has the symbolization delivered an implicit message? It is in the treatment of Rome as distinct, but essentially equivalent, to the former kingdoms of Babylonia, Media, and Greece. This seems to me a stunning way of saying that the now-Christian empire in no way requires differentiation from its pagan predecessors. Nothing has changed, except matters have gotten worse. Beyond Rome, standing in a straight line with the others, lies the true shift in history, the rule of Israel and the cessation of the dominion of the (pagan) nations.

Leviticus Rabbah came to closure, it is generally agreed, around 400 c.e., that is, approximately a century after the Roman Empire in the east had begun to become Christian, and half a century after the last attempt to rebuild the Temple in Jerusalem had failed — a tumultuous age indeed. Accordingly, we have had the chance to see how distinctive and striking are the ways in which the symbols of animals that stand for the four successive empires of humanity and point toward the messianic time serve the framers' message. We see rabbinic Midrash as allegory and parable, such as *Leviticus Rabbah*. We may then contrast rabbinic Midrash as allegory and Midrash as paraphrase on the one hand, and prophecy on the other.

10

Midrash and Numbers:
Two Approaches

To this point, readers may imagine that rabbinic Midrash is essentially uniform and everywhere allegorical. For we have noticed that the same composition may serve two writers to make pretty much the same points about salvation, as in the case of *Genesis Rabbah* and *Leviticus Rabbah*. But that impression should be balanced by another. Rabbinic Midrash reveals diverse approaches to the labor of interpretation, and allegory is only one of them. When we compare what one writer thinks important about a verse of Scripture with what another writer, of the same religious world and of approximately the same period, chooses to emphasize in that same verse of Scripture, we must conclude that in hand are the results of the exegesis of different people talking about different things to different people.[1]

Specifically, we shall read a single verse from the Book of Numbers as it is treated in two Midrash-documents, one interested in the expansion of the verse through secondary paraphrase, the other engaged in a far-reaching exercise of allegory. By comparing the work of the writers of two Midrash-compilations, we see that, while paramount, parabolic or allegorical Midrash represented only one approach to Midrash-processes.

To appreciate the range of rabbinic Midrash, therefore, we take up the exercise introduced in chapter 2, that of *comparative Midrash*.[2] Comparing exegeses of the same theme or verse of Scripture among the

---

1. Compare my "The Jewish Christian Argument in the First Century. Different People Talking about Different Things to Different People," *Crosscurrents* 35 (1985): 148–58.

2. See my *Comparative Midrash: The Plan and Program of Genesis Rabbah and Leviticus Rabbah*, Brown Judaic Studies (Atlanta: Scholars Press, 1986).

same circles of exegetes rests on solid foundations in logic.[3] Two documents in the same canon surely bear broad affinities, having been selected by the consensus of the sages or the faithful as authoritative. They rely upon the opinion or judgment of sages of the same circle. They have been preserved and handed on by the same institutions of the faith. They presumably present basically cogent convictions upon the meaning of Scripture. Accordingly, a variety of indicators justifies the judgment that the documents form a solid fit, bearing much in common. Then, it must follow, the work of comparison yields to the exercise of contrast. Being alike, the documents, in their treatment of precisely the same verse of Scripture, produce differences. And these differences make a difference. They tell us how one writer wishes to read Scripture in one way, another in a different way. In the case at hand, however, the differences prove so profound and far-reaching that they call into question the very act of comparison.

In this exercise, we compare the treatment of precisely the same verse by exegetes within the same religious world. One writer produced *Sifré to Numbers*, a systematic, verse-by-verse reading of the Book of Numbers. We have no reliable date for this Midrash-compilation, though the late third or early fourth century seems possible (ca. 300). The other stands behind *Pesiqta de Rab Kahana*, a collection of syllogisms pertinent to the holy days of the synagogue calendar. A fair guess on the date of that document will place it after *Leviticus Rabbah* (i.e., after ca. 450 C.E.) but before the Talmud of Babylonia (ca. 600). In their shared reading of Num. 7:1, *"On the day when Moses had finished setting up the tabernacle . . . ,"* we see strikingly different approaches to what is important in the verse. Indeed, as we shall see, it is difficult to relate the message of the one to that of the other.

That is a surprising result, since we have every reason to expect people who read Scripture within pretty much the same framework to observe similar points of stress in the same passage. But that is not what we shall now see. Indeed, were the theory to take shape that within the circles of the sages of the dual Torah were profound differences on what required stress and what did not, the following comparison of exegeses — comparative Midrash — would provide solid evidence. Quite how to sort out the amazing differences in approach, emphasis, and inquiry that separate the authorship of *Sifré to Numbers* from that of *Pesiqta de Rab Kahana* remains a puzzle. I am here raising the question of how both

---

3. Compare Jonathan Z. Smith, "What a Difference a Difference Makes," in *"To See Ourselves as Others See Us": Jews, Christians, "Others" in Late Antiquity*, ed. Jacob Neusner and Ernest S. Frerichs (Atlanta: Scholars Press, 1985), 3–48.

documents belong within the same canon and asking what we can mean by canon when the authoritative writings relate so slightly as do these.

SIFRÉ TO NUMBERS

All the named authorities in *Sifré to Numbers* belong to the age of the Mishnah, but we have no way of identifying the authentic from the pseudepigraphic attributions. In the model of the Tosefta,[4] a demonstrably Amoraic document, which cites verbatim and comments on the Mishnah and so is post-Mishnaic, we may hardly assign *Sifré to Numbers* to a period before the end of the fourth century.[5] It makes use of two basic approaches. First, the syllogistic composition, which rests on the premise that Scripture supplies hard facts that, properly classified, generate syllogisms. By collecting and classifying facts of Scripture, therefore, we may produce firm laws of history, society, and Israel's everyday life. The second maintains the fallibility of reason unguided by scriptural exegesis. Scripture alone supplies reliable basis for speculation. Laws cannot be generated by reason or logic unguided by Scripture. That is the recurrent polemic of the document — a point of interest completely outside of the imagination of the framers of *Pesiqta de Rab Kahana.* Both documents are arguing about different things, presumably with different people. For nothing in the questions addressed to the Book of Numbers draws one group into alignment with the other: they simply do not raise the same questions or produce congruent answers. Whether or not the exegetical-eisegetical results can be harmonized is a separate question.[6]

Sifré to Numbers XLIV:I[7]

1

A. *"On the day when Moses had finished setting up the tabernacle [and had anointed and consecrated it with all its furnishings and had anointed and consecrated the altar with all its utensils, the leaders of Israel, heads of their fathers' houses, the leaders of the tribes, who were over those who were numbered, offered and brought their offerings before the Lord, six covered wagons and*

---

4. I have demonstrated that fact in my systematic comparison of the Tosefta to the Mishnah in my *History of the Mishnaic Law* (Leiden: Brill, 1974–86), I–XLIII, and in my *Tosefta: Translated from the Hebrew,* vols. 1–6 (New York: Ktav, 1977–86).

5. Moses David Herr, "Midrash," *Encyclopaedia Judaica* (Jerusalem: Keter, 1971). I have found no more authoritative statement on the present view of the dates of all Midrash-compilations than Herr's. It is a question that will have to be reopened in time.

6. That question demands attention in a far wider context than the present one. For it is the issue that when addressed will require us to ask what we mean by the canon, and, more important, what meanings inhere within the canon as a whole but not in some one of its parts — what holds the whole together that is not stated in any one component? I have no doubt whatever that that Judaism behind the systems of the several components of the canon of the dual Torah awaits systematic and rigorous definition; but at this writing I am uncertain about how to proceed.

7. All translations in this chapter are by the author.

twelve oxen, a wagon for every two of the leaders, and for each one an ox, they offered them before the tabernacle. Then the Lord said to Moses, 'Accept these from them, that they may be used in doing the service of the tent of meeting, and give them to the Levites, to each man according to his service.' So Moses took the wagons and the oxen and gave them to the Levites]" (Num. 7:1-6):

B. Scripture indicates that for each of the seven days of consecrating the tabernacle, Moses would set up the tabernacle, and every morning he would anoint it and dismantle it. But on that day he set it up and anointed it, but he did not dismantle it.

C. R. Yose b. R. Judah: "Also on the eighth day he set it up and dismantled it, for it is said, *'And in the first month in the second year of the first day of the month the tabernacle was erected'* (Exod. 30:17). On the basis of that verse we learn that on the twenty-third day of Adar, Aaron and his sons, the tabernacle and the utensils were anointed."

The focus of interest is the meaning of the word KLH or KLT, that is, "completed," and the same point will be made in *Pesiqta de Rab Kahana*. But here it is the main point, since the exegete proposes to say what he thinks the simplest sense of the verse is. The second compilation of exegeses, by contrast, treats the matter in a much richer and more imaginative way.

Sifré to Numbers XLV:I

2

A. On the first day of the month the tabernacle was set up, on the second the red cow was burned [for the purification rite required at Numbers 19], on the third day water was sprinkled from it, in lieu of the second act of sprinkling, and the Levites were shaved.

B. On that same day the Presence of God rested in the tabernacle, as it is said, *"Then the cloud covered the tent of meeting, and the glory of the Lord filled the tabernacle, and Moses was not able to enter the tent of meeting, because the cloud abode upon it"* (Exod. 40:34).

C. On that same day the heads offered their offerings, as it is said, *"He who offered his offering the first day . . ."* (Num. 7:12). Scripture uses the word "first" only in a setting when "first" introduces all of the days of the year.

D. On that day fire came down from heaven and consumed the offerings, as it is said, *"And fire came forth from before the Lord and consumed the burnt offering and the fat upon the altar"* (Lev. 9:24).

E. On that day the sons of Aaron offered strange fire, as it is said, *"Now Nadab and Abihu, the sons of Aaron, each took his censer and put fire in it . . . and offered unholy fire before the Lord, such as he had not commanded them"* (Lev. 10:1).

F. *"And they died before the Lord . . ."* (Lev. 10:2): they died before the Lord, but they fell outside [of the tabernacle, not imparting corpse uncleanness to it].

G. How so? They were on their way out.

H. R. Yose says, "An angel sustained them, as they died, until they got out, and they fell in the courtyard, as it is said, *'And Moses called Mishael and Elzaphan, the sons of Uzziel the uncle of Aaron, and said to them, "Draw near,*

71

carry your brethren from before the sanctuary out of the camp" (Lev. 10:4). What is stated is not, 'From before the Lord,' but, 'from before the sanctuary.' "

I. R. Ishmael says, "The context indicates the true state of affairs, as it is said, 'And they died before the Lord,' meaning, they died inside and fell inside. How did they get out? People dragged them with iron ropes."

The exegete draws together a broad range of events which, in his view, all took place on one day. But what is interesting is what he does not say. He does not introduce the issue of Israel and Israel's redemption. Rather, he focuses upon the here and the now of what happened long ago. There is a perceived difference between the one-time historical event of the setting up of the tabernacle and the eternal and paradigmatic character of the event: its continuing meaning, not its one-time character of all. The tabernacle is not the paradigm of the natural world, and Israel's salvation simply plays no role in the passage.

The expansion and amplification of the base verse runs through no. 1. From that point, no. 2, we deal with the other events of that same day, surveying the several distinct narratives which deal with the same thing, Exodus 40, Leviticus 9 — 10, and so on. This produces the effect of unifying the diverse scriptural accounts into one tale, an important and powerful exegetical result. One of the regular contributions of these exegetes is to collect and harmonize a diversity of verses taken to refer to the same day, event, or rule.

Sifré to Numbers XLIV:II

1

A. "*. . . and had anointed and consecrated it with all its furnishings and had anointed and consecrated the altar with all its utensils*":

B. Might I infer that as each utensil was anointed, it was sanctified?

C. Scripture says, "*. . . and had anointed and consecrated it with all its furnishings and had anointed and consecrated the altar with all its utensils*," meaning that not one of them was sanctified until all of them had been anointed. [The process proceeded by stages.]

Once more we shall see that the second exegesis, that of *Pesiqta de Rab Kahana*, makes precisely this point. But it is swallowed up in a much different range of interest. It covers nearly everything in *Sifré to Numbers*, but makes nothing of what is constitutive of the received writing.

PESIQTA DE RAB KAHANA

The formal traits of the second compilation to treat Num. 7:1ff. differ radically from those of the first. *Pisiqta de Rab Kahana* falls into precisely the same structural-formal classification as *Genesis Rabbah* and *Leviticus Rabbah*. It approaches the exegesis of the verse of primary interest, the base verse, by means of a secondary and superficially unrelated verse, the intersecting verse. The latter will be extensively treated, entirely on its own. Then the exegete will move from the intersecting verse to the base verse, showing how the verse chosen from some other passage in fact opens up the deeper meaning of the verse of primary concern.

In what follows the intersecting verse, Song 5:1, is chosen because it refers to "bride," and the word for "had finished" is formed on the letters KLH, which can be read as "bride." So in the mind of the exegete an appropriate intersecting verse will speak of the same matter — KLH = "finish" or "bride"— and the rest follows. But that intersecting verse imparts its deepest meaning on the base verse, and, in the present instance, the tabernacle on that account is taken as the place in which Israel entered the bridal canopy of God. The clear purpose of the writer emerges in the treatment of the base verse, Num. 7:1: teleological-eschatological, referring to the beginning, middle, and end. The one thing important about the base verse is the opposite of the main thing that struck the writer of *Sifré to Numbers:* its interest in a one-time event on a particular day. To the writer of *Pesiqta de Rab Kahana,* Scripture presents eternal paradigms and not one-time history.

Pesiqta de Rab Kahana I:I

1

A. *"I have come back to my garden, my sister, my bride"* (Song 5:1):

B. R. Azariah in the name of R. Simon said, "[The matter may be compared to the case of] a king who became angry at a noble woman and drove her out and expelled her from his palace. After some time he wanted to bring her back. She said, 'Let him renew in my behalf the earlier state of affairs, and then he may bring me back.'

C. "So in former times the Holy One, blessed be he, would receive offerings from on high, as it is said, *'And the Lord smelled the sweet odor'* (Gen. 8:21). But now he will accept them down below."

2

A. *"I have come back to my garden, my sister, my bride"* (Song 5:1):

B. Said R. Hanina, "The Torah teaches you proper conduct,

C. "specifically, that a groom should not go into the marriage canopy until the bride gives him permission to do so: *'Let my beloved come into his garden'* (Song 4:16), after which, *'I have come back to my garden, my sister, my bride'* (Song 5:1)."

The intersecting verse (Song 5:1) is fully exposed entirely on its own terms, before we are able to recover the base verse (Num. 7:1) and find out what we learn about that verse from the intersecting one.

Pesiqta de Rab Kahana I:I

3

A. R. Tanhum, son-in-law of R. Eleazar b. Abina, in the name of R. Simeon b. Yosni: "What is written is not, 'I have come into the garden,' but rather, '*I have come back to my garden.*' That is, 'to my [Mandelbaum:] canopy.'

B. "That is to say, to the place in which the principal [presence of God] had been located to begin with.

C. "The principal locale of God's presence had been among the lower creatures, in line with this verse: '*And they heard the sound of the Lord God walking about*' (Gen. 3:8)."

6

A. [Reverting to 3.C,] the principal locale of God's presence had been among the lower creatures, but when the first man sinned, it went up to the first firmament.

B. The generation of Enosh came along and sinned, and it went up from the first to the second.

C. The generation of the flood [came along and sinned], and it went up from the second to the third.

D. The generation of the dispersion . . . and sinned, and it went up from the third to the fourth.

E. The Egyptians in the time of Abraham our father [came along] and sinned, and it went up from the fourth to the fifth.

F. The Sodomites . . . , and sinned . . . from the fifth to the sixth.

G. The Egyptians in the time of Moses . . . from the sixth to the seventh.

H. And, corresponding to them, seven righteous men came along and brought it back down to earth:

I. Abraham our father came along and acquired merit, and brought it down from the seventh to the sixth.

J. Isaac came along and acquired merit and brought it down from the sixth to the fifth.

K. Jacob came along and acquired merit and brought it down from the fifth to the fourth.

L. Levi came along and acquired merit and brought it down from the fourth to the third.

M. Kahath came along and acquired merit and brought it down from the third to the second.

N. Amram came along and acquired merit and brought it down from the second to the first.

O. Moses came along and acquired merit and brought it down to earth.

P. Therefore it is said, "*On the day that Moses completed the setting up of the tabernacle, he anointed and consecrated it*" (Num. 7:1).

The selection of the intersecting verse, Song 5:1, rests, as I said, on the appearance of the letters KLH or KLT, meaning "completed," but yielding also the word KLH, meaning "bride." The exegete wishes to make the point that in building the tabernacle, Moses has brought God down to earth (6.P). This he accomplishes by bringing the theme of "garden, bride" together with the theme of the union of God and Israel. The parable at 1.B then is entirely apt, since it wishes to introduce the notion of God's having become angry with humanity but then reconciled through Israel in the sacrificial cult. Number 1.B then refers to the fall from grace, with Israel as the noble spouse who insists that the earlier state of affairs be restored. Number 1.C then makes explicit precisely what is in mind, a very effective introduction to the whole. Number 2 pursues the exegesis of the intersecting verse, as does no. 3, the latter entirely apropos. Number 6 then brings us back to 3.C, citing the language of the prior component and then making the point of the whole quite explicit. Even with the obvious accretions at nos. 4, 5, the whole hangs together and makes its point — the intersecting verse Song 5:1, the base verse Num. 7:1 — in a cogent way. We now take up the *base verse* in its own terms.

Pesiqta de Rab Kahana I:V

1

A. Another interpretation of the verse: *"On the day that Moses completed the setting up of the tabernacle, he anointed and consecrated it"* (Num. 7:1):

B. The letters translated as "completed" are so written that they be read "bridal", that is, on the day on which [Israel, the bride] entered the bridal canopy.

2

A. R. Eleazar and R. Samuel bar Nahmani:

B. R. Eleazar says, " *'On the day that Moses completed'* means on the day on which he left off setting up the tabernacle day by day."

C. It has been taught on Tannaite authority: Every day Moses would set up the tabernacle, and every morning he would make his offerings on it and then take it down. On the eighth day [to which reference is made in the verse, *'On the day that Moses completed the setting up of the tabernacle, he anointed and consecrated it'*] he set it up but did not take it down again.

D. Said R. Zeira, "On the basis of this verse we learn that fact that an altar set up on the preceding night is invalid for the offering of sacrifices on the next day."

E. R. Samuel bar Nahmani says, "Even on the eighth day he set it up and took it apart again."

F. And how do we know about these dismantlings?

G. It is in line with what R. Zeira said, " *'On the day that Moses completed'* means on the day on which he left off setting up the tabernacle day by day."

3

A. R. Eleazar and R. Yohanan:

B. R. Eleazar said, " *'On the day that Moses completed'* means on the day on which demons ended their spell in the world.

C. "What is the Scriptural basis for that view?

D. " *'No evil thing will befall you, nor will any demon come near you by reason of your tent'* (Ps. 91:10) — on the day on which demons ended their spell in the world."

E. Said R. Yohanan, "What need do I have to derive the lesson from another passage? Let us learn it from the very passage in which the matter occurs: *'May the Lord bless you and keep you'* (Num. 6:24) — keep you from demons."

4

A. R. Yohanan and R. Simeon b. Laqish:

B. R. Yohanan said, " *'On the day that Moses completed'* means on the day on which hatred came to an end in the world. For before the tabernacle was set up, there was hatred and envy, competition, contention, and strife in the world. But once the tabernacle was set up, love, affection, comradeship, righteousness, and peace came into the world.

C. "What is the verse of Scripture that so indicates?

D. " *'Let me hear the words of the Lord, are they not words of peace, peace to his people and his loyal servants and to all who turn and trust in him? Deliverance is near to those who worship him, so that glory may dwell in our land. Love and fidelity have come together, justice and peace join hands'* " (Ps. 85:8–10).

E. Said R. Simeon b. Laqish, "What need do I have to derive the lesson from another passage? Let us learn it from the very passage in which the matter occurs: *'and give you peace.'* "

5

A. *'[On the day that Moses completed]* the setting up of the Tabernacle, *[he anointed and consecrated it]'* ":

B. R. Joshua b. Levi in the name of R. Simeon b. Yohai: "What is stated is not 'setting up the tabernacle [without the accusative particle, *et*],' but 'setting up + *the accusative particle* + the tabernacle,' [and since the inclusion of the accusative particle is taken to mean that the object is duplicated, we understand the sense to be that he set up a second tabernacle along with the first].

C. "What was set up with it? It was the world that was set up with [the tabernacle, that is, the tabernacle represented the cosmos].

D. "For until the tabernacle was set up, the world trembled, but after the tabernacle was set up, the world rested on firm foundations."

We work our way through the clause, *"on the day that Moses completed."* Number 1 goes over familiar ground. It is a valuable review of the point of stress, the meaning of the word "completed." Number 2 refers to the claim that from day to day Moses would set up and take down the tent, until on the day at hand, he left it standing; so the "completed" bears the sense of ceasing to go through a former procedure. The word under study bears the further sense of "coming to an end," and therefore at nos. 3, 4, we ask what came to an end when the tabernacle was set up. The matched units points to demons on the one side, and hatred on the other.

76

Pesiqta de Rab Kahana I:VII

1

A. *"The chief men of Israel, heads of families — that is, the chiefs of the tribes,* [*who had assisted in preparing the detailed lists*] — *came forward and brought their offering before the Lord"* (Num. 7:2):

B. [The word for "tribes" can mean "rods," so we understand the meaning to be they had exercised authority through rods] in Egypt.

C. *". . . who had assisted in preparing the detailed lists"* — the standards.

The clause-by-clause interpretation of the base verse (Num. 7:2) does not vastly differ in intent from the interpretation generated by leading the intersecting verse (Exod. 26:6, 11) into the base verse. That is to say, in both cases we have a highly allusive and wide-ranging reading, in which we construct meanings deriving from eternal categories, not one-time events but paradigms, as I said earlier. That trait of the exegetical-eisegetical mind of the later document emerges most strikingly in what follows.

2

A. *". . . came forward and brought their offering before the Lord, six covered wagons [and twelve oxen, one wagon from every two chiefs and from each one an ox]"* (Num. 7:2):

B. The six corresponded to the six days of creation.

C. The six corresponded to the six divisions of the Mishnah.

D. The six corresponded to the six matriarchs: Sarah, Rebecca, Rachel, Leah, Bilhah, and Zilpah.

E. Said R. Yohanan, "The six corresponded to the six religious duties that pertain to a king: *'He shall not have too many wives'* (Deut. 17:17), *'He shall not have too many horses'* (Deut. 17:16), *'He shall not have too much silver and gold'* (Deut. 17:17), *'He shall not pervert justice, show favor, or take bribes'* (Deut. 16:9)."

3

A. The six corresponded to the six steps of the throne. How so?

B. When he goes up to take his seat on the first step, the herald goes forth and proclaims, *"He shall not have too many wives"* (Deut. 17:17).

C. When he goes up to take his seat on the second step, the herald goes forth and proclaims, *"He shall not have too many horses"* (Deut. 17:16).

D. When he goes up to take his seat on the third step, the herald goes forth and proclaims, *"He shall not have too much silver and gold"* (Deut. 17:17).

E. When he goes up to take his seat on the fourth step, the herald goes forth and proclaims, *"He shall not pervert justice."*

F. When he goes up to take his seat on the fifth step, the herald goes forth and proclaims, *". . . show favor."*

G. When he goes up to take his seat on the sixth step, the herald goes forth and proclaims *". . . or take bribes"* (Deut. 16:9).

H. When he comes to take his seat on the seventh step, he says, "Know before whom you take your seat."

4

A. *"And the top of the throne was round behind"* (1 Kings 10:19):

B. Said R. Aha, "It was like the throne of Moses."

C. *"And there were arms on either side of the throne by the place of the seat"* (1 Kings 10:19):

D. How so? There was a scepter of gold suspended from behind, with a dove on the top, and a crown of gold in the dove's mouth, and he would sit under it on the Sabbath, and it would touch but not quite touch.

5

A. The six corresponded to the six firmaments.

B. But are they not seven?

C. Said R. Abia, "The one where the King dwells is royal property [not counted with what belongs to the world at large]."

We proceed with the detailed exposition of Num. 7:2. The focus of interest, after no. 1, is on the reason for bringing six wagons. The explanations, nos. 2 (+ 3–4), 5, relate to the creation of the world, the Torah, the life of Israel, the religious duties of the king, and the universe above. The underlying motif, the tabernacle as the point at which the supernatural world of Israel meets the supernatural world of creation, is carried forward.

It seems superfluous at this point to observe that the one group of exegetes has virtually nothing in common with the other, even though, at some few points, the exegetes of *Pesiqta de Rab Kahana* go over ground covered by those in *Sifré to Numbers.* What one set of sages wishes to know in the verse of Scripture at hand scarcely coincides with the program of the other. The comparison of Midrashim in this case yields a picture of differences so profound as to call into question the premise with which we started, which is that the writers of the two documents derive from the same movement, share the same viewpoint, and therefore exhibit sufficient traits in common to justify our comparing the exegetical results of the one with those of the other. Once we undertake the comparison we find nothing in common — nothing.

The upshot is that the two writers go their respective ways. One has little to say to the other. They may be characterized as different people talking about different things to different people. That is because the approach of each set of exegetes to the base verse derives from its own clearly defined program of inquiry. That program imposes its issues on the base verse but scarcely responds to the base verse. Accordingly, these are purposeful documents. They do more than merely assemble this and that, forming a hodgepodge of things people happen to have said. In the case of each document we can answer the question: Why this, not that?

They are not compilations but compositions; seen as a group, therefore, they are not essentially the same. Each expresses its viewpoint. Both have presented not a scrapbook but a statement.

These documents of the oral Torah's exegesis of the written Torah emerge as rich in differences from one another and sharply defined — each through its distinctive viewpoints and particular polemics on the one side, and formal and aesthetic qualities on the other. We deal with a canon, yes, but with a canon made up of highly individual documents. But that, after all, is what a canon is — a mode of classification that takes a library and turns it into a cogent, if composite, statement. A canon comprises separate books that all together make a single statement. In terms of the Judaism of the dual Torah, the canon is what takes Scriptures of various kinds and diverse points of origin and turns Scriptures into Torah, and turns commentaries on those scriptures into Torah as well, making them all into the one whole Torah — of Moses, our rabbi.

Allegory and Proposition 1:
The Fall of Adam and
The Rise of Israel

We now turn to Midrash-processes and their propositional results. For the allegorical or parabolic reading of Scripture served rabbinic Midrash in theological, not primarily literary, ways. The midrashists intended to prove certain propositions which were meant to function as syllogisms: once proved, they could generate their own, further statements, each standing for many other facts of Israel's salvation. In order to highlight the syllogistic argument constructed through an allegorical reading of Scripture, I take up three syllogisms. All concern Israel's redemption and salvation. We see how Scripture, in sages' hands, turned into a powerfully persuasive mode of argument in support of an urgent message to the contemporary age. The proofs called upon the facts of Scripture that, for sages and for Israel at large, served much as did the facts of nature and of logic did for natural philosophy in the Greek tradition. That is, proposition came under the test of fact, and facts could prove syllogisms or disprove them.

The first of the three propositions of salvation concerns the meaning of human history. Due to the world-historical changes of the fourth century, both Christian and Judaic theologians had to rethink everything from the beginning to the present. Just as Eusebius, in creating Christian history, turned to Adam to interpret the most current events, so sages reread Genesis for the same purpose.

In the case of proposition 1, sages wish to argue that the fall of Adam marked the rise of Israel. For what the sages' reading of Scripture accomplished was to account for the human condition in drawing the contrast between their sad present, dominated by the children of Adam, and the hopeful future beyond their time, which would be shaped by the children of Israel. This argument then formed a counterweight to the appeal of the first Christian historians, beginning with Eusebius, to the same facts of creation. By allegorical Midrash, therefore, sages read the narrative of creation and the fall of Adam to testify to the redemption, rise, and salvation of Israel. We begin with a single example of the syllogistic proposition and then offer a more general statement of it.

A cogent and uniform world view, one that generated the allegorical reading to begin with, accompanied our sages when they approached the text of Genesis. Their world view they systematically joined to the Genesis text, fusing the tale at hand with that larger context of imagination in which the tale was received and read.[1] Accordingly, when we follow the sages' mode of interpreting Genesis, we find our way deep into their imaginative life. Scripture becomes the set of facts that demonstrate the truth of the syllogisms that encompassed and described the world, as the sages saw it. The thesis of this systematic and polemical midrashic reading is that Israel's salvific history over centuries subsequent to creation informs and infuses the creation of the world in Genesis 1–20. That ancient story takes on its true meaning from what has happened to Israel, and it follows that Israel's future history accounts for the creation of the world.

Genesis Rabbah XX:I[2]

1

A. *"Then the Lord God said to the serpent, 'Because you have done this, cursed are you above all cattle and above all wild animals' "* (Gen. 3:14):

B. *"A slanderer shall not be established in the earth; the violent and wicked man shall be hunted with thrust upon thrust"* (Ps. 140:12).

C. Said R. Levi, "In the world to come the Holy One, blessed be he, will take the nations of the world and bring them down to Gehenna. He will say to them, 'Why did you impose fines upon my children?'

D. "They will say to him, 'Some of them slandered others among them.'

E. "The Holy One, blessed be he, will then take these [Israelite slanderers] and those and bring them down to Gehenna."

2

A. Another interpretation: "A slanderer" refers to the snake, who slandered his creator.

B. *"Will not be established* [standing upright] *on earth:"* *"Upon your belly you shall go"* (Gen. 3:14).

C. *"The violent and wicked man shall be hunted:"* What is written is not "with a thrust" but *"with thrust after thrust,"* [since not only the serpent was cursed]. What is written is "thrust after thrust," for man was cursed, woman was cursed, and the snake was cursed.

D. *"And the Lord God said to the serpent . . ."*

---

1. See my *Genesis and Judaism: The Perspective of Genesis Rabbah* (Atlanta: Scholars Press, 1986).
2. All translations in this chapter are by the author.

We have an exegesis of a base verse (Gen. 3:14) and an intersecting verse (Ps. 140:12) in that "classic" form in which the intersecting verse is fully worked out and only then drawn to meet the base verse. Number 1 treats the intersecting verse as a statement on its own, and then no. 2 reads the verse in line with Gen. 3:14. But the intersecting verse is hardly chosen at random, since it speaks of slander in general, and then at no. 2 the act of slander of the snake is explicitly read into the intersecting verse. So the intersection is not just thematic. The upshot of the exercise links Israel's history to the history of humanity in the Garden of Eden. Number 1 focuses upon the sacred history of Israel, making the point that slanderers in Israel cause the nation's downfall, just as the snake caused the downfall of humanity. In what follows we trace the fall of humanity from Adam and Eve, the rise of humanity from Abraham, Isaac, Jacob upward to Sinai:

Genesis Rabbah XIX:VII

2

A. ["*And they heard the sound of the Lord God walking in the garden in the cool of the day*" (Gen 3:8):] Said R. Abba bar Kahana, "The word is not written 'move,' but rather 'walk,' bearing the sense that [the Presence of God] leapt about and jumped upward.

B. "[The point is that God's presence leapt upward from the earth on account of the events in the garden, as will now be explained:] The principal location of the Presence of God was [meant to be] among the creatures down here. When the first man sinned, the Presence of God moved up to the first firmament. When Cain sinned, it went up to the second firmament. When the generation of Enosh sinned, it went up to the third firmament. When the generation of the flood sinned, it went up to the fourth firmament. When the generation of the Dispersion [at the Tower of Babel] sinned, it went up to the fifth. On account of the Sodomites it went up to the sixth, and on account of the Egyptians in the time of Abraham it went up to the seventh.

C. "But, as a counterpart, there were seven righteous men who rose up: Abraham, Isaac, Jacob, Levi, Kahath, Amram, and Moses. They brought the Presence of God [by stages] down to earth.

D. "Abraham brought it from the seventh to the sixth, Isaac brought it from the sixth to the fifth, Jacob brought it from the fifth to the fourth, Levi brought it down from the fourth to the third, Kahath brought it down from the third to the second, Amram brought it down from the second to the first. Moses brought it down to earth."

E. Said R. Isaac, "It is written, '*The righteous will inherit the land and dwell therein forever*' (Ps. 37:29). Now what will the wicked do? Are they going to fly in the air? But that the wicked did not make it possible for the Presence of God to take up residence on earth [is what the verse wishes to say]."

What is striking is the claim that while the wicked (Gentiles) drove God out of the world, the righteous (Israelites) brought God back into the world. Sages link the story of the fall of man to the rise of Israel, with Israel serving as the counterpart and fulfillment of the Fall at creation. Now the fall of Adam is tied to the history of Israel:

Genesis Rabbah XIX:IX

1

A. *"And the Lord God called to the man and said to him, 'Where are you?' "* (Gen. 3:9):

B. [The word for "where are you" yields consonants that bear the meaning,] "How has this happened to you?"

C. [God speaks:] "Yesterday it was in accord with my plan, and now it is in accord with the plan of the snake. Yesterday it was from one end of the world to the other [that you filled the earth], and now: *'Among the trees of the garden'* (Gen. 3:8) [you hide out]."

2

A. R. Abbahu in the name of R. Yose bar Haninah: "It is written, *'But they are like a man [Adam], they have transgressed the covenant'* (Hosea 6:7).

B. "'They are like a man,' specifically, like the first man.

We shall now compare the story of the first man in Eden with the story of Israel in its land. Here is vintage allegory:

C. "'In the case of the first man, I brought him into the Garden of Eden, I commanded him, he violated my commandment, I judged him to be sent away and driven out, but I mourned for him, saying, "How . . ." [which begins the Book of Lamentations, hence stands for a lament, but which, as we just saw, also is written with the consonants that also yield, 'Where are you?'].

D. "'I brought him into the Garden of Eden,' as it is written, *'And the Lord God took the man and put him into the Garden of Eden'* (Gen. 2:15).

E. "'I commanded him,' as it is written, *'And the Lord God commanded . . .'* (Gen. 2:16).

F. "'And he violated my commandment,' as it is written, *'Did you eat from the tree concerning which I commanded you?'* (Gen. 3:11).

G. "'I judged him to be sent away,' as it is written, *'And the Lord God sent him from the garden of Eden'* (Gen. 3:23).

H. "'And I judged him to be driven out.' *'And he drove out the man'* (Gen. 3:24).

I. " *But I mourned for him, saying, "How . . .".* '*And he said to him, "Where are you?"* ' (Gen. 3:9), and the word for 'where are you?' is written, 'How . . .'

J. " 'So too in the case of his descendants, [God continues to speak,] I brought them into the Land of Israel, I commanded them, they violated my commandment, I judged them to be sent out and driven away but I mourned for them, saying, "How . . ." '

K. " *'I brought them into the Land of Israel.' 'And I brought you into the land of Carmel'* (Jer. 2:7).

L. " *'I commanded them.' 'And you, command the children of Israel'* (Exod. 27:20). *'Command the children of Israel'* (Lev. 24:2).

M. " 'They violated my commandment.' 'And all Israel have violated your Torah' (Dan. 9:11).

N. " 'I judged them to be sent out.' 'Send them away, out of my sight and let them go forth' (Jer. 15:1).

O. " '. . . and driven away.' 'From my house I shall drive them' (Hosea 9:15).

P. " 'But I mourned for them, saying, "How . . ." ' 'How has the city sat solitary, that was full of people?' (Lam. 1:1)."

I find deeply moving both treatments of Gen. 3:9. Israel's history forms the counterpart to Adam's. Israel then is humanity incarnate. Number 1 simply contrasts one day with the next, a stunning and stark statement, lacking all decoration. It sets the stage for no. 2 and the whole must be regarded as a thoughtful composition. The other, no. 2, similarly compares the story of man in the Garden of Eden with the tale of Israel in its Land. Every detail is in place, the articulation is perfect, and the result completely convincing as an essay in interpretation. All of this rests on the simple fact that the word for "where are you?" may be expressed as "How . . . ," which invokes the opening words of the Book of Lamentations. So Israel's history serves as a paradigm for human history, and vice versa. But there is a difference between Israel and Adam. Israel obeys God's Word, and Adam did not, so Israel will be saved, as Adam fell. The contrast of Adam and Israel is drawn once more:

Genesis Rabbah XXI:VII

3

A. Judah b. Pedaiah interpreted, "Who will remove the dust from between your eyes, O first man! For you could not abide in the commandment that applied to you for even a single hour, and lo, your children can wait for three years to observe the prohibition of the use of the fruit of a tree for the first three years after it is planted: *Three years shall it be as forbidden to you, it shall not be eaten'* (Lev. 19:23)."

B. Said R. Huna, "When Bar Qappara heard this, he said, 'Well have you expounded matters, Judah, son of my sister!' "

Number 3 compares the character of Israel to the character of the first man, calling Israel "descendants of the first man" and pointing out that they can observe a commandment for a long time. The example is apt, since Israel observes the prohibition involving the fruit of a newly planted tree, and does so for three years, while the first man could not keep his hands off a fruit tree for even an hour. Israel's history — the course from Abraham onward to the end of time — thus forms the counterpart to the history of humanity. Adam was the first human being, and Israel was the counterpart and opposite. The anthropology then is clear: there is unredeemed Adam and holy Israel. This is shown in the claim that while the first man could not do what God demanded, Israel can and does do God's will. We come now to a simple and clear statement of the main point of it all:

Genesis Rabbah LXXXIII:V

1

A. Wheat, straw, and stubble had a fight.

B. Wheat said, "It was on my account that the field was sown."

C. Stubble said, "It was on my account that the field was sown."

D. Wheat said, "The day will come and you will see."

E. When the harvest time came, the householder began to take the stubble and burn it, and the straw and spread it, but the wheat he made into heaps.

F. Everyone began to kiss the wheat. [I assume this is a reference to the messianic passage, "Kiss the son," which is also to be translated, "Kiss the wheat" (Ps. 2:12).]

G. So too Israel and the nations of the world have a fight.

H. These say, "It was on our account that the world was created," and those say, "It was on our account that the world was created."

I. Israel says, "The day will come and you will see."

J. In the age to come: "You shall fan them and the wind will carry them away" (Isa. 41:16).

K. As to Israel: "And you shall rejoice in the Lord, you shall glory in the Holy One of Israel" (Isa. 41:16).

The particular proof text before us, important in Christian exegesis as proof that Jesus Christ is son of God, makes its point in a rather poignant way. Finally, the sages make explicit their basic view: the world was created for Israel, and not for the nations of the world. At the end of time everyone will see what only Israel now knows. When, at the outset, I described rabbinic Midrash as an exercise in demonstrating that things are not what they seem to be, readers will agree, I did not exaggerate.

12

Allegory and Proposition 2: "Comfort, comfort my people, says your God"

In reading one thing in light of others and finding beneath the surface a reality that superficially escapes our vision, the framers of Midrash in general present propositions in two ways. First, they may repeatedly revert to a single allegory, finding the four monarchies in diverse biblical statements and stories, for instance. The allegory then yields its message like a set-piece tableau: the four monarchies yield to the fifth, which is that of Israel, and Israel's rule is coming. That syllogism emerges from a variety of tableaus, but is stated in a clear way in only a few of them. We see, therefore, that Midrash can produce important propositions not cogently spelled out. Another instance of the same rather diffuse and luxurious mode of expression has just impressed us. The proposition that in Adam's fall Israel rose to glory does not emerge in a single passage and is not the sole theme of the portion of the document in which it occurs. For *Genesis Rabbah* covers a variety of topics and in so doing presents a range of diverse propositions.

Pesiqta de Rab Kahana, by contrast, argues in a cogent way on behalf of a single syllogism; it is left implicit but is everywhere paramount. Among the documents of the fifth century, produced in the aftermath of the religious crisis of the fourth, *Pesiqta de Rab Kahanna* (see chap. 10) provides among the Midrash-compilations the single most cogent statement of whatever points it wishes to make. This is done in two ways, just as we saw earlier. First, the framers will choose a base verse, to be repeated, and they will then produce an intersecting verse. In the collision of the two verses a meaning emerges. That meaning can be clearly stated and forms the implicit syllogism of the entire chapter at hand. Second, the framers will interpret the components of the base verse one by one, and they will systematically read their implicit syllogism into the elements of that base verse. In these two ways they leave no doubt about the point they wish to make as well as about the absolute validity of that point.

The proposition handsomely presented in *Pesiqta de Rab Kahana Pisqa* XVI argues the syllogism that God is righteous and that God will certainly — because of that righteousness — save Israel. The base verse cited at the end, 8.C, is Isa. 40:1, *"Comfort, comfort my people, says your God,"* and the intersecting verse (Job 4:17–20) makes the point that mortal man cannot be more righteous than God, and Israel must therefore have perfect confidence that God being righteous will save Israel. That syllogism is expressed by the contrast of Job 4:17–20 and Isa. 40:1, then repeated in a variety of other ways, both through intersections with the base verse and through systematic rereading of components of that base verse.

Pesiqta de Rab Kahana XVI:I[1]

1

A. *"Can mortal man be more righteous than God, or the creature purer than his maker? [If God mistrusts his own servants and finds his messengers at fault, how much more those that dwell in houses whose walls are clay, whose foundations are dust, which can be crushed like a bird's nest, or torn down between dawn and dark, how much more shall such men perish outright and unheeded, die without ever finding wisdom?]"* (Job 4:17–20):

B. Now can there be a man more righteous than his creator?

C. But one's deeds purify a person.

D. Said the Holy One, blessed be he, "Boaz brings comfort, should I not bring comfort?"

2

A. Boaz brings comfort: *"Boaz answered, 'It has certainly been told to me [all that you have done for your mother-in-law since your husband's death, how you left your father and mother, and the land of your birth and came to a people you did not know before yesterday or the day before yesterday. The Lord reward your deed; may the Lord the God of Israel, under whose wings you have come to take refuge, give you all that you deserve']"* (Ruth 2:11–12).

B. Why is the verb for "tell" repeated two times? ["Certainly been told" is a translation of the Hebrew repetition the verb "told" twice for emphasis.]

C. He said to her, "It has been told to me in the household, and it has been told to me in the field."

D. *". . . all that you have done for your mother-in-law since your husband's death":* and it goes without saying, during the lifetime of your husband.

E. *". . . how you left your father and mother":* your actual parents.

F. *". . . and the land of your birth":* this refers to your neighborhood.

---

1. All translations in this chapter are by the author.

3

A. Another interpretation: *". . . how you left your father and mother"*: this refers to your idolatry: *". . . saying to a piece of wood, You are my father, and to stone, You have given birth to me"* (Jer. 2:27).

B. *". . . and the land of your birth"*: this refers to your own town.

4

A. *". . . and came to a people you did not know before yesterday or the day before yesterday"*:

B. He said to her, "If you had come to us yesterday or the day before yesterday, we should not have accepted you, for the law governing the Amonites had not yet been renewed, prohibiting a male Amonite, but not a female, a male Moabite but not a female."

5

A. *"The Lord reward your deed: [may the Lord the God of Israel, under whose wings you have come to take refuge, give you all that you deserve]"*:

B. He said to her, "He who is destined to pay a reward to the righteous will pay your reward."

C. *". . . give you all that you deserve"*:

D. What is written for the sense, *"all that you deserve,"* is spelled to be read "Solomon."

E. Said R. Yose, "He said to her, Solomon will descend from you."

6

A. *". . . May the Lord the God of Israel, under whose wings you have come to take refuge"*:

B. Said R. Abun, "The earth has wings, the dawn has wings, the sun has wings, the cherubs have wings, the heavenly creatures have wings, the seraphim have wings.

C. "The earth has wings: *'From the wings of the earth we have heard songs'* (Isa. 24:16).

D. ". . . the dawn has wings: *'I went up on the wings of dawn'* (Ps. 139:9).

E. ". . . the sun has wings: *'But to you who fear my name shall the sun of righteousness arise with healing in its wings'* (Mal. 3:20).

F. ". . . the cherubs have wings: *'And the sound of the wings of the cherubim'* (Ezek. 10:5).

G. ". . . the heavenly creatures have wings: *'The noise of the wings of the living creatures'* (Ezek. 3:13).

H. ". . . the seraphim have wings: *'Above him stood the seraphim. Each one of them had six wings'* (Isa. 6:2)."

I. Said R. Abun, "Great is the power of those who deal mercifully, for they take shelter not in shadow of the wings of the earth nor in the shadow of the wings of the dawn, nor in the shadow of the wings of the sun, nor in the shadow of the wings of the cherubs, nor in the shadow of the wings of the heavenly creatures, nor in the shadow of the wings of the seraphim.

J. "In the shadow of whom do they take refuge? In the shadow of the Holy One, blessed be he, as it is written, *'Precious is the lovingkindness ordained by you, O God. Because of it the children of men take refuge in the shadow of your wings'* (Ps. 36:7)."

88

7

A. She said, " 'Indeed sir, you have eased my mind [and spoken kindly to me; may I ask you as a favor not to treat me only as one of your slave-girls?' When meal-time came around,] Boaz said to her, '[Come here and have something to eat, and dip your bread into the sour wine.' So she sat beside the reapers, and he passed her some roasted grain. She ate all she wanted and still had some left over]" (Ruth 2:13–14):

B. "He said to her, 'Do not speak in such a way, that you have been counted among the slave-girls, you are counted only among the matriarchs.' "

8

A. [Reverting to 1.D: Said the Holy One, blessed be he, "Boaz brings comfort, should I not bring comfort?"] Lo, it is an argument a fortiori:

B. Now, if Boaz, who spoke words of goodness and comfort to the heart of Ruth, comforted her, when the Holy One, blessed be he, comes to comfort Jerusalem, how much the more so:

C. "Comfort, comfort my people, says your God. [Speak tenderly to Jerusalem and cry to her that her warfare is ended, that her iniquity is pardoned, that she has received from the Lord's hand double for all her sins]" (Isa. 40:1–2).

The interesting point of stress comes at the end, that God will be the one to comfort Jerusalem, as the base verse says. The interesting question is how the intersecting verse contributes, since it is not cited. But the answer is obvious: Can mortal man be more righteous than God, or the creature purer than his maker? If Boaz comforts Ruth, then God will surely comfort Jerusalem. The selection of Ruth, of course, is not difficult to explain. She is the mother of the Messiah, functioning in Judaism like Mary in Christianity. The entire passage therefore is an essay on the coming of the Messiah to comfort Israel, the Jewish people, in its time of tribulation. If we did not know how profound a shock was made by the Christianization of the ruling empire, Rome, the recurrent passages of the present kind would made us guess that something had called into question Israel's sense of its future redemption. Then sages' recurrent stress would have pointed toward a situation of doubt and despair.

Pesiqta de Rab Kahana XVI:VIII

1

A. "How will you comfort me through vanity, and as for your answers, there remains only faithlessness" (Job 21:34):

B. Said R. Abba bar Kahana [on the meaning of the word translated as "faithlessness"], "Your words [of comfort and consolation, that Job's friends had provided him] require clarification."

C. Rabbis say, "Your words contain contradictions." [We shall now have a long series of examples of how God's messages to the prophets contradict themselves.]

2

A. The Holy One said to the prophets, "Go and comfort Jerusalem."

B. Hosea went to give comfort. He said to her [the city], "The Holy One, blessed be he, has sent me to you to bring you comfort."

C. She said to him, "What do you have in hand?"

D. He said to her, *"I will be as the dew to Israel"* (Hosea 14:6).

E. She said to him, "Yesterday, you said to me, *'Ephraim is smitten, their root is dried up, they shall bear no fruit'* (Hosea 9:16), and now you say this to me? Which shall we believe, the first statement or the second?"

3

A. Joel went to give comfort. He said to the city, "The Holy One, blessed be he, has sent me to you to bring you comfort."

B. She said to him, "What do you have in hand?"

C. He said to her, *"It shall come to pass in that day that the mountains shall drop down sweet wine and the hills shall flow with milk"* (Joel 4:18).

D. She said to him, "Yesterday, you said to me, *'Awake you drunkards and weep, wail, you who drink wine, because of the sweet wine, for it is cut off from your mouth'* (Joel 1:5), and now you say this to me? Which shall we believe, the first statement or the second?"

4

A. Amos went to give comfort. He said to the city, "The Holy One, blessed be he, has sent me to you to bring you comfort."

B. She said to him, "What do you have in hand?"

C. He said to her, *'On that day I will raise up the fallen tabernacle of David'* (Amos 9:11).

D. She said to him, "Yesterday, you said to me, *'The virgin of Israel is fallen, she shall no more rise'* (Amos 5:2), and now you say this to me? Which shall we believe, the first statement or the second?"

5

A. Micah went to give comfort. He said to the city, "The Holy One, blessed be he, has sent me to you to bring you comfort."

B. She said to him, "What do you have in hand?"

C. He said to her, *"Who is like God to you who pardons iniquity and passes by transgression?"* (Micah 7:18).

D. She said to him, "Yesterday, you said to me, *'For the transgression of Jacob is all this and for the sins of the house of Israel'* (Micah 1:56), and now you say this to me? Which shall we believe, the first statement or the second?"

6

A. Nahum went to give comfort. He said to the city, "The Holy One, blessed be he, has sent me to you to bring you comfort."

B. She said to him, "What do you have in hand?"

C. He said to her, *"The wicked one shall no more pass through you, he is utterly cut off"* (Nahum 2:1).

D. She said to him, "Yesterday, you said to me, *'Out of you came he forth who devises evil against the Lord, who counsels wickedness'* (Nahum 1:11), and now you say this to me? Which shall we believe, the first statement or the second?"

7

A. Habakkuk went to give comfort. He said to the city, "The Holy One, blessed be he, has sent me to you to bring you comfort."

B. She said to him, "What do you have in hand?"

C. He said to her, *"You have come forth for the deliverance of your people, for the deliverance of your anointed"* (Hab. 3:13).

D. She said to him, "Yesterday, you said to me, *'How long, O Lord, shall I cry and you will not hear, I cry to you of violence'* (Hab. 1:22), and now you say this to me? Which shall we believe, the first statement or the second?"

8

A. Zephaniah went to give comfort. He said to the city, "The Holy One, blessed be he, has sent me to you to bring you comfort."

B. She said to him, "What do you have in hand?"

C. He said to her, *"It shall come to pass at that time that I will search Jerusalem with the lamps"* (Zeph. 1:12).

D. She said to him, "Yesterday, you said to me, *'A day of darkness and gloominess, a day of clouds and thick darkness'* (Zeph. 1:15), and now you say this to me? Which shall we believe, the first statement or the second?"

9

A. Haggai went to give comfort. He said to the city, "The Holy One, blessed be he, has sent me to you to bring you comfort."

B. She said to him, "What do you have in hand?"

C. He said to her, *"Shall the seed ever again remain in the barn? Shall the vine, the fig tree, the pomegranate, and the olive tree ever again bear no fruit? Indeed not, from this day I will bless you"* (Hag. 2:19).

D. She said to him, "Yesterday, you said to me, *'You sow much and bring in little'* (Hag. 1:6), and now you say this to me? Which shall we believe, the first statement or the second?"

10

A. Zechariah went to give comfort. He said to the city, "The Holy One, blessed be he, has sent me to you to bring you comfort."

B. She said to him, "What do you have in hand?"

C. He said to her, *"I am very angry with the nations that are at ease"* (Zech. 1:15).

D. She said to him, "Yesterday, you said to me, *'The Lord was very angry with your fathers'* (Zech. 1:2), and now you say this to me? Which shall we believe, the first statement or the second?"

11

A. Malachi went to give comfort. He said to the city, "The Holy One, blessed be he, has sent me to you to bring you comfort."

B. She said to him, "What do you have in hand?"

C. He said to her, *"All the nations shall call you happy, for you shall be a happy land"* (Mal. 3:12).

D. She said to him, "Yesterday, you said to me, *'I have no pleasure in you, says the Lord of hosts'* (Mal. 1:10), and now you say this to me? Which shall we believe, the first statement or the second?"

12

A. The prophets went to the Holy One, blessed be he, saying to him, "Lord of the ages, Jerusalem has not accepted the comfort [that we brought her]."

B. Said to them the Holy One, blessed be he, "You and I together shall go and comfort her."

C. Thus we say: *"Comfort, comfort my people"* but read the letters for "my people" as "with me."

D. Let the creatures of the upper world comfort her, let the creatures of the lower world comfort her.

E. Let the living comfort her, let the dead comfort her.

F. Comfort her in this world, comfort her in the world to come.

G. Comfort her on account of the Ten Tribes, comfort her on account of the tribe of Judah and Benjamin.

H. [Thus we must understand the statement, *"Comfort, comfort my people, says your God. Speak tenderly to the heart of Jerusalem and cry to her that her warfare is ended, that her iniquity is pardoned, that she has received from the Lord's hand double for all her sins"* (Isa. 40:1-2) in this way:] *"Comfort, comfort my people"* but read the letters for "my people" as "with me."

This sustained, remarkably powerful exercise in contrasting contradictory statements of the prophets yields a stunning revision of the message of the base verse (Isa. 40:1-2): God and the angels and all beings assemble to comfort Jerusalem. I cannot point to an equivalently sustained and effective composition in the whole of canonical literature. Through the tableau, through the dialectical movement of exegesis, through the repeated demonstration of the same point, the basic proposition is both displayed and demonstrated: God will save Israel. It is an amazing achievement, when we notice that nowhere does anyone tell us the proposition concerning salvation that everyone wishes to prove. We conclude with one example of the exegesis of the base verse in its own terms, now no longer with reference to an intersecting verse at all.

Pesiqta de Rab Kahana XVI:IX

1

A. [With reference to the base verse, *"Comfort, comfort my people, [says your God. Speak tenderly to the heart of Jerusalem and cry to her that her warfare is ended, that her iniquity is pardoned, that she has received from the Lord's hand double for all her sins]"* (Isa. 40:1-2)] R. Abin made two statements.

B. R. Abin said, "The matter may be compared to the case of a king who had a palace. His enemies invaded it and burned it. Who has to be comforted, the palace or the owner of the palace? Is it not the owner of the palace?

C. "Thus said the Holy One, blessed be he, 'The house of the sanctuary is my house, as it is written, *"On account of my house, which has been destroyed"* (Hag. 1:9). Who then has to be comforted? Is it not I?'

D. "So it follows: 'Comfort, comfort, my people,' means 'Comfort me, comfort me, my people.' "

2

A. R. Abin made a second statement.

B. R. Abin said, "The matter may be compared to the case of a king who had a vineyard. His enemies invaded it and cut it down and laid it waste. Who has to be comforted, the vineyard or the owner of the vineyard? Is it not the owner of the vineyard?

C. "Thus said the Holy One, blessed be he, 'Israel is my vineyard, "For the vineyard of the Lord of hosts is the house of Israel" (Isa 5:7). Who then has to be comforted? Is it not I?'

D. "So it follows: 'Comfort, comfort my people,' means 'Comfort me, comfort me, my people.' "

3

A. R. Berekhiah made two statements, one in his own name and one in the name of R. Levi.

B. R. Berekhiah said, "The matter may be compared to the case of a king who had a flock. Wolves invaded the flock and decimated it. Who has to be comforted, the flock or the owner of the flock? Is it not the owner of the flock?

C. "Thus said the Holy One, blessed be he, 'Israel is my flock: "And I put my flock, the flock of my pasture . . ." (Ezek. 34:31). Who then has to be comforted? Is it not I?'

D. "So it follows: 'Comfort, comfort my people,' means 'Comfort me, comfort me, my people.' "

4

A. R. Berekhiah made a statement in the name of R. Levi: "The matter may be compared to the case of a king who had a vineyard and handed it over to a sharecropper.

B. "When the vineyard produced good wine, he would say, 'How good is the wine of my vineyard!' But when it produced bad wine, he would say, 'How bad is the wine of my sharecropper['s vineyard]!'

C. "That sharecropper said to him, 'My lord, O king, whether it is good or bad, it's yours!'

D. "So to begin with, the Holy One, blessed be he, said to Moses, 'Now go, I shall send you to Pharaoh, and bring out my people, the children of Israel from Egypt' (Exod. 3:10).

E. "But when they committed that deed [of the golden calf], what is written? 'Go, descend, for your people has corrupted . . .' " (Exod. 32:7).

F. "Said Moses before the Holy One, blessed be he, 'Lord of the ages, when they sin, they are mine, but when they are guiltless, they are yours? Not so! Whether they sin or whether they are guiltless, they are yours.'

G. "For it is written, 'And they are your people and your inheritance' (Deut. 9:29), 'Do not destroy your people and your inheritance' (Deut. 9:26), 'Why is the Lord angry with your people' (Exod. 32:11), 'why are you going to destroy your people?' "

H. Said R. Simon, "[Moses] did not desist from speaking with love of them until [God] had called them, My people: 'For the Lord regretted the evil which he had thought of doing to his people' (Exod. 32:14)."

The three parallel parables yield a climactic one at the end, which makes the same point in a different, and still more effective way. The people is always *"my people,"* as the base verse says. That general observation is restated at the end not as a parable but as an exercise in the juxtaposition of texts, a separate mode of discourse. Other passages will stress the future consolation of Israel, as against the view that the rebuilding of the second Temple fulfilled the prophetic promises and there would be no future consolation for Israel. The final point is that, however Israel sinned, Israel was punished in due measure and will be comforted in precisely the same measure.

13

Allegory and Proposition 3: Proof That the Resurrection of the Dead Is a Scriptural Doctrine

The proving of propositions through Midrash-exegesis took place not only implicitly but also explicitly. In such exercises, the passage will state its question: How do we know on the basis of Scripture that . . . , and then the proposition to be tested against the scientific evidence of Scripture will be spelled out. Then Scripture serves to prove that stated propositions of the Mishnah or of the oral Torah in general conform to and derive from the written Torah. When, therefore, we wish to understand how rabbinic Midrash proposes to read one thing in light of some other, we have to follow the Midrash-exegetes as they demonstrate the presence in verses of the written Torah of propositions paramount in the oral Torah. The single most sustained and interesting such exercise brings our survey of the rabbinic Midrash as allegory (or parable) to a close. For once we can show that one thing really contains within itself another thing, we have attained our purpose. In this case, we wish to show that the oral Torah contains a truth that is also to be found in the written Torah or Scripture. In this way the fundamental mode of thought and interpretation represented by rabbinic Midrash has reached its full statement and accomplished its entire purpose. Allegory and parable in literary form express the generative theological truth of the Judaism of the dual Torah, and that is why they serve.

At issue here is the proposition in the Mishnah (*m. Sanhedrin* 11:1-2) that all Israelites have a portion in the world to come. Of concern in the immediate literary context is the implicit conviction that the dead rise up and live, and that conviction is now to be linked to verses of Scripture. For among those who will not enjoy the resurrection of the dead and eternal life are people who do not find that belief in Scripture. By treating Scripture as allegory once more one sustains a proposition that

Scripture is unlikely to validate if it is read in a different way. Thus we may conclude that wherever a proof text is cited for a proposition not explicitly stated in Scripture, the mode of thought that deems said proof text probative rests upon an allegorical or parabolic hermeneutic: this proves that, because this really means or stands for that.

We begin with the Mishnah-paragraph to which the Talmud of Babylonia appends its sustained proofs, of which I give only a sample, that Scripture — not solely the oral Torah — maintains that the dead are resurrected and live in eternal life. The Mishnah is presented in boldface type, and verses of Scripture, as usual, in italics.[1]

Mishnah-tractate Sanhedrin 11:1

A. All Israelites have a share in the world to come,

B. as it is said, *"Your people also shall be all righteous, they shall inherit the land forever; the branch of my planting, the work of my hands, that I may be glorified"* (Isa. 60:21).

C. And these are the ones who have no portion in the world to come:

D. He who says, the resurrection of the dead is a teaching which does not derive from the Torah, and the Torah does not come from Heaven; and an Epicurean.

We now take up the systematic exposition of the passage at hand, with stress on the proposition that Scripture indeed sustains the belief in the resurrection of the dead. If one does not accept the belief that the Torah teaches, one cannot gain the advantage of that doctrine.

Babylonian Talmud Tractate Sanhedrin 90A

I

A. Why all this [that is, why deny the world to come to those listed]?

B. On Tannaite authority [it was stated], "Such a one denied the resurrection of the dead, therefore he will not have a portion in the resurrection of the dead.

C. "For all the measures [meted out by] the Holy One, blessed be he, are in accord with the principle of measure for measure."

D. For R. Samuel bar Nahmani said R. Jonathan said, "How do we know that all the measures [meted out by] the Holy One, blessed be he, accord with the principle of measure for measure?

E. "As it is written, *'Then Elisha said, Hear you the word of the Lord. Thus says the Lord, Tomorrow about this time shall a measure of fine flour be sold for a shekel, and two measures of barley for a shekel in the gates of Samaria'* (2 Kings 7:1).

F. "And it is written, *'Then a lord on whose hand the king leaned answered the man of God and said, Behold, if the Lord made windows in heaven, might this thing be? And he said, Behold, you shall see it with your eyes, but shall not eat thereof'* (2 Kings 7:2).

G. [**90B**] "And it is written, *'And so it fell unto him; for the people trod him in the gate and he died'* (2 Kings 7:20).

1. All translations in this chapter are by the author.

96

H. But perhaps it was Elisha's curse that made it happen to him, for R. Judah said Rab said, "The curse of a sage, even for nothing, will come about."

I. If so, Scripture should have said, "They trod upon him and he died." Why say, *"They trod upon him in the gate"*?

J. It was on account of matters pertaining to [the sale of wheat and barley at] the gate [which he had denied, that he died].

The basic notion of divine justice has now been introduced, and we proceed to the case at hand: Scripture's numerous proofs that the dead will rise on judgment day.

II

A. How, on the basis of the Torah, do we know about the resurrection of the dead?

B. As it is said, *"And you shall give thereof the Lord's heave-offering to Aaron the priest"* (Num. 18:28).

C. And will Aaron live forever? And is it not the case that he did not even get to enter the Land of Israel, from the produce of which heave-offering is given?

D. Rather, this teaches that he is destined once more to live, and the Israelites will give him heave-offering.

E. On the basis of this verse, therefore, we see that the resurrection of the dead is a teaching of the Torah.

The first proof for our syllogism sets the model for the rest. The proof is this: we adduce in evidence a verse that presupposes that, at some point in the future, a biblical figure will be alive. Since we know that that person is now dead, we can only surmise that Scripture's implicit syllogism maintains that the dead will rise — or, at least, that person in particular. We skip some secondary amplification of the foregoing and come directly to the next exercise.

IV

A. It has been taught on Tannaite authority:

B. R. Simai says, "How on the basis of the Torah do we know about the resurrection of the dead?

C. "As it is said, *'And I also have established my covenant with [the patriarchs] to give them the land of Canaan'* (Exod. 6:4).

D. " 'With you' is not stated, but rather, 'with them,' indicating on the basis of the Torah that there is the resurrection of the dead."

We have the same argument for the same syllogism, merely a different case, proved as the premise of argument requires, by scriptural evidence.

V

A. *Minim* [Jewish heretics, sometimes thought to be Jewish Christians] asked Rabban Gamaliel, "How do we know that the Holy One, blessed be he, will resurrect the dead?"

B. He said to them [directing their attention to Scripture in particular, rather than to arguments based on natural philosophy], "It is proved from the Torah, from the Prophets, and from the Writings." But they did not accept his proofs.

C. "From the Torah: for it is written, *'And the Lord said to Moses, Behold, you shall sleep with your fathers and rise up'* (Deut. 31:16)."

D. They said to him, "But perhaps the sense of the passage is, *'And the people will rise up'* (Deut 31:16)?"

E. "From the Prophets: as it is written, *'Thy dead men shall live, together with my dead body they shall arise. Awake and sing, you that live in the dust, for your dew is as the dew of herbs, and the earth shall cast out its dead'* (Isa. 26:19)."

F. "But perhaps that refers to the dead whom Ezekiel raised up."

G. "From the Writings, as it is written, *'And the roof of your mouth, like the best wine of my beloved, that goes down sweetly, causing the lips of those who are asleep to speak'* (Song 7:9)."

H. "But perhaps this means that the dead will move their lips?"

I. That would accord with the view of R. Yohanan.

J. For R. Yohanan said in the name of R. Simeon b. Yehosedeq, "Any authority in whose name a law is stated in this world moves his lips in the grave,

K. "as it is said, *'Causing the lips of those that are asleep to speak.'* "

L. [The *minim* would not concur in Gamaliel's view] until he cited for them the following verse: " *'Which the Lord swore to your fathers to give to them'* (Deut 11:21) — to them and not to you, so proving from the Torah that the dead will live."

M. And there are those who say that it was the following verse that he cited to them: " *'But you who cleaved to the Lord you God are alive, everyone of you this day'* (Deut. 4:4). Just as on this day all of you are alive, so in the world to come all of you will live."

The more systematic proof derives from all three divisions of Scripture (Torah, Prophets, Writings), and the narrative setting underlines the contentious character of the proposition. The notion that Midrash rests on allegory in the deepest sense — finding in Scripture something that is not explicitly stated but is in the profound layers of Scripture's meaning — is illustrated time and again. We note that the outsider does not ask the question before us, which is the Scriptural basis for the belief, but the sage always draws upon verses of Scripture to prove the point. The same phenomenon follows: the Romans/Aramaeans (the manuscript evidence is never firm on this point) ask Joshua a question in general terms, "how do we know," and he answers, "because Scripture says." In that exchange in humble details lies the center and heart of rabbinic Midrash-exegesis: all knowledge derives from or can be shown implicit in Scripture!

VI

A. Romans asked R. Joshua b. Hananiah, "How do we know that the Holy One will bring the dead to life and also that he knows what is going to happen in the future?"

B. He said to them, "Both propositions derive from the following verse of Scripture:

C. "As it is said, 'And the Lord said to Moses, Behold you shall sleep with your fathers and rise up again, and this people shall go awhoring . . .' (Deut. 31:16)."

D. "But perhaps the sense is, '[the people] will rise up and go awhoring' "

E. He said to them, "Then you have gained half of the matter, that God knows what is going to happen in the future."

This exchange is somewhat unsatisfying, since the sage does not complete the required proof — for the outsider. But the insider understands that he has given a fine and solid answer. And if we were to miss that point, precisely the same answer to the correctly framed question is now repeated.

VII

A. It has also been stated on Amoraic authority:

B. Said R. Yohanan in the name of R. Simeon b. Yohai, "How do we know that the Holy One, blessed be he, will bring the dead to life and knows what is going to happen in the future?

C. "As it is said, 'Behold, you shall sleep with your fathers, and . . . rise again . . .' (Deut. 31:16)."

We cannot miss the simple point that Joshua's proof text serves quite well, despite the unsatisfactory conclusion above.

VIII

A. It has been taught on Tannaite authority:

B. Said R. Eliezer b. R. Yose, "In this matter I proved false the books of the minim.

C. "For they would say, 'The principle of the resurrection of the dead does not derive from the Torah.'

D. "I said to them, 'You have forged your Torah and have gained nothing on that account.'

E. "For you say, 'The principle of the resurrection of the dead does not derive from the Torah.' "

F. "'Lo, Scripture says, "[Because he has despised the word of the Lord . . .] that soul shall be cut off completely, his iniquity shall be upon him" (Num. 15:31).

G. "'. . . shall be utterly cut off . . . ,'" in this world, in which case, at what point will '. . . his iniquity be upon him . . .'?

H. " 'Will it not be in the world to come?' "

I. Said R. Pappa to Abayye, "And might one not have replied to them that the words 'utterly . . .' '. . . cut off . . . ,' signify the two worlds [this and the next]?"

J. [He said to him,] "They would have answered, 'The Torah speaks in human language [and the doubling of the verb carries no meaning beyond its normal sense].' "

IX

A. This accords with the following Tannaite dispute:

B. " 'That soul shall be utterly cut off'—'shall be cut off'— in this world, 'utterly'— in the world to come," the words of R. Aqiba.

C. Said R. Ishmael to him, "And has it not been said, 'He reproaches the Lord, and that soul shall be cut off' (Num. 15:31)? Does this mean that there are three worlds?

D. "Rather: '. . . it will be cut off . . . ,' in this world, '. . . utterly . . . ,' in the world to come, and 'utterly cut off . . . ,' indicates that the Torah speaks in ordinary human language."

E. Whether from the view of R. Ishmael or of R. Aqiba, what is the meaning of the phrase, "his iniquity shall be upon him"?

F. It accords with that which has been taught on Tannaite authority:

G. Is it possible that that is the case even if he repented?

H. Scripture states, "his iniquity shall be upon him."

I. I have made the statement at hand only for a case in which "his iniquity is yet upon him" [but not if he repented].

The next corollary requires that we treat the resurrection not in the context of scriptural proof but topical rationality. It is simply to maintain that the dead will live.

XII

A. A Tannaite authority of the house of R. Ishmael [taught], "[Resurrection] is a matter of an argument a fortiori based on the case of a glass utensil.

B. "Now if glassware, which is the work of the breath of a mortal man, when broken, can be repaired,

C. "A mortal man, who is made by the breath of the Holy One, blessed be he, how much the more so [that he can be repaired, in the resurrection of the dead]."

We conclude with controversy stories, between sages and *minim* — commonly understood to be Jewish heretics — on the question of the resurrection of the dead. We note that familiar themes now recur within a fresh setting.

XIII

A. A *min* said to R. Ammi, "You say that the dead will live. But they are dust, and will the dust live?"

B. He said to him, "I shall draw a parable for you. To what may the matter be compared?

C. "It may be compared to the case of a mortal king, who said to his staff, 'Go and build a great palace for me, in a place in which there is no water or dirt [for bricks].'

D. "They went and built it, but after a while it collapsed.

E. "He said to them, 'Go and rebuild it in a place in which there are dirt and water [for bricks].'

F. "They said to him, 'We cannot do so.'

G. "He became angry with them and said to them, 'In a place in which there is neither water nor dirt you were able to build, and now in a place in which there are water and dirt, how much the more so [should you be able to build it]!'

H. "And if you [the *min*] do not believe it, go to a valley and look at a rat, which today is half-flesh and half-dirt and tomorrow will turn into a creeping thing, made all of flesh. Will you say that it takes much time? Then go up to a mountain and see that today there is only one snail, but tomorrow it will rain and the whole of it will be filled with snails."

We conclude where we began by acknowledging the genius of rabbinic Midrash as the reading of Scripture in an allegorical or parabolic way, so as to turn Scripture from a picture of what it seems to say into an account of what it really means. This ultimate meaning, the point and the payoff of the allegory, insists on the union of Israel's present sanctification and its coming salvation. In all that we have read in the rabbinic Midrash-compilations, the propositions of the Midrash-exegeses repeatedly come down to this one claim.

Salvation and sanctification join together in Midrash in the Judaism of the dual Torah. The laws of the Pentateuch, focused as they are on the sanctification of the nation through its cult, indicate the rules of salvation as well in Midrash in the Judaism of the dual Torah. The message of Midrash in the Judaism of the dual Torah attaches itself to the Pentateuchal books such as Leviticus or Numbers or Deuteronomy, as if those books had come from prophecy and addressed the issue of the meaning of history and Israel's salvation. But the Pentateuch came in its final form from the priesthood and spoke of sanctification.

The paradoxical syllogism — the as-if-reading, the Midrash-process that sees Scripture's message as the very opposite of how things seem — therefore reaches simple formulation. In the very setting of Pentateuchal law with its stress on Israel's sanctification we find the promise of salvation. In the topics of the cult and the priesthood we uncover the national and social issues of the moral life and redemptive hope of Israel. The repeated comparison and contrast of priesthood and prophecy, sanctification and salvation, turn out to produce a complement, which comes to most perfect union. So much for mind and intellect, the realm of Midrash in word. But Scripture speaks from heart to heart, from soul to soul, in works of imagination, not only in words of truth and faith. Midrash partakes of symbol that transcends verbal explanation and evokes that reality of meaning that relies not on words but on the response of soul to soul and heart to heart and spirit to spirit. When the Word speaks to the world, it is not alone in words that the message comes, and not mainly in words that the world responds.

Epilogue

It remains to articulate the meaning of Midrash, as worked out in the Judaism of the dual Torah, for religious people (Jews and Christians alike) in the world today. Midrash shows us how the Judaic sages mediated between God's Word and their own world, equally and reciprocally invoking the one as a metaphor for the other. They learned from Scripture about what it meant for humanity to be "in our image, after our likeness," and they learned in the difficult world in which they lived how life in God's image of humanity, as Scripture set forth that image, was to be not only endured but lived in full holiness. It was to be the godly life on earth (in the language of Judaism), God incarnate in Jesus Christ (in the language of Christianity), life as the imitation of God (in language shared by both). In concrete terms, in the Midrash we Jews see not "the Old Testament" or "the Hebrew Bible" but the one whole Torah, oral and written, that is Judaism. And, in the model of Matthew (and not Matthew alone) Christians receive Scripture as the principal component of the gospel of Jesus Christ. These twin affirmations unite us. In that dual Torah, but also in that gospel of the incarnate God, Scripture, read in the prism of Midrash, forms a commentary on everyday life — as much as everyday life brings with it fresh understanding of Scripture.

That theological conviction moreover frames a theology of culture, one that constantly refers to Scripture in the interpretation of everyday life, and to everyday life in the interpretation of Scripture. Such a theology of culture invokes both the eternal and continuing truths of Scripture and also the ephemeral but urgent considerations of the here and now. Midrash then forms that bridge, defines that metaphor, holds in the balance those two worlds of the here and now and the always. It reads the one in the light of the other, imparting one meaning to both, drawing each toward the plane of the other. Midrash reads the everyday as the metaphor against which the eternal is to be read, and the eternal as the metaphor against which the everyday is to be reenacted. In this fact I find a theological method pertinent to tomorrow's theologies of both Judaism and Christianity.

Here I want to emphasize that there is a constant interplay, an ongoing interchange, between everyday affairs and the word of God in the Torah — Scripture. What we see reminds us of what Scripture says — and what Scripture says informs our understanding of the things we see and do in everyday life. That is what, in my view, the critical verse of Scripture, "In all thy ways, know him," means. And the deep structure of human existence, framed by Scripture and formed out of God's will as spelled out in the Torah, forms the foundation of our everyday life. Here and now, in the life of the hour, we can and do know God. So everyday life forms a commentary on revealed Scripture — on the Torah — and Scripture, the Torah, provides a commentary on everyday life. Life flows in both directions.

Seen theologically, therefore, Midrash thus holds together two competing truths, first, the authority of Scripture, and, second, that equally ineluctable freedom of interpretation implicit in the conviction that Scripture speaks now, not only then. Joining the two, each in balance and proper proportion, Midrash as the process of mediation between the Word of God in Scripture and the world in which we live and serve realizes the continuity, in the here and now, of the original revealed Torah/Testament. Forming a profoundly conservative and constructive power in the cultural and political life of Israel (the Jewish people), Midrash legitimates innovation in the name of the received revelation, while preserving the vitality and ongoing pertinence of revelation in the present age. Eternity in time comes to realization in the processes of Midrash, which, through literary means, define a sacred society, a consecrated culture.

Now let me spell this out in terms of the samples of Midrash we have surveyed. The founders of Judaism as we know it, who flourished in the first seven centuries C.E., brought Scripture into their world and their world into Scripture. They therefore show us how people shaped their understanding of the world out of the resources of God's revelation of the beginnings of humanity, and, especially, of God's people, Israel. The great sages, honored with the title of rabbi, transformed the Torah into a plan and design for the world, the everyday as an instance of the eternal. They read Scripture as God's picture of creation and humanity.

103

They read the life of the streets and marketplaces, the home and the hearth, the nations and the world, as an ongoing commentary on Scripture and the potentialities (not all of them good) of creation. So, as I said, Torah flows in both directions.

The world reveals not chaos but order (cosmos), and God's will — the order of the world — works itself out not once but again and again. That is the meaning of God's order for the world. If — the Judaic sages in Midrash maintained — sages could find out how things got going, they might also find meaning in today and method in where they were heading. That is why they looked to a reliable account of the past and searched out the meaning of their own days. They form a model for our Midrash too. To give one concrete example: bringing to the stories of Genesis the conviction that the Book of Genesis told not only the story of yesterday but also the tale of tomorrow, the sages transformed a picture of the past into a prophecy for a near tomorrow. That transformation constitutes Midrash, whether of the Book of Genesis or, in the later trends in the rabbinic Bible interpretation, of the text of the sacred calendar of the synagogue itself. And we can do no less.

The sages therefore present us with a model — therefore also a theological program for culture — of how through Midrash people mediated between the received and the givens of their own time. In the written Torah they hoped to find, and they did find, the story of the day at hand, which they anticipated would indeed form the counterpart and conclusion to the story of beginnings. From creation to conclusion, from the beginnings of salvation in the patriarchs and matriarchs to the ending of salvation and its fulfillment in their own day — this is what our sages sought to discover. Midrash as parable, but also as paraphrase and prophecy, shows us how Israel's sages, Essene, Christian, rabbinic, among many kinds and families in ancient times read Scripture in light of their own concerns — but then listened carefully to the teachings of the Torah about contexts like their context, and circumstances such as those they faced.

They exercised a freedom of interpretation by insisting that God speaks through the Torah to Israel everywhere and continually. But when they brought to the written Torah the deepest anguish of the age, they allowed that component of the Torah to speak to them in the here and now. The bridge they built brought traffic in both directions, from today to Sinai, from Sinai to the present moment. That is what I mean when I present Midrash as mediator. The principal mode of thinking in Midrash translates the metaphor into a policy of culture, for it requires us to look deeply at something, for in the depths we find something else (things are not what they seem) — always in the depths of God's revealed will in the Torah. And that account of the continuity of culture under the aspect of Midrash leads us to the limits of this world, which mark the bottom boundary and the threshold of the other.

Glossary

INTRODUCTION TO TALMUDIC AND MIDRASHIC WRITINGS

The Mishnah is a philosophical law code, produced in the Land of Israel ("Palestine") in ca. 200 C.E. The first Talmud to the Mishnah was formed in the Land of Israel in ca. 400 C.E., and is called "the Talmud of the Land of Israel" or "the Jerusalem Talmud," and in Hebrew "the Yerushalmi." This Talmud covers thirty-nine of the Mishnah's sixty-two tractates. The second Talmud to that same Mishnah was created in Babylonia, which corresponds to present-day Iraq, around Baghdad, in ca. 600 C.E. and is called "the Talmud of Babylonia," and in Hebrew "the Bavli." Both Talmuds to the one Mishnah consist of a series of citations of Mishnah-paragraphs and systematic, carefully drafted explanations of words and phrases of the Mishnah-passage, followed by secondary expansions of principles of the Mishnah-passage.

A brief account of the writings between the Mishnah and the Bavli will place into context the authoritative and conclusive statement of the whole. The writings of the sages between the Mishnah and the Bavli, ca. 200 and 600 C.E., fall into two distinct groups, one beginning with the Mishnah and ending about two centuries later, in 400, with the Tosefta and close associates of the Mishnah; the other beginning with the Yerushalmi in ca. 400 C.E. and ending about two centuries later with the Bavli. The Mishnah, as we know, drew in its wake tractate *Abot*, a statement concluded a generation after the Mishnah on the standing of the authorities of the Mishnah. Attached to the Mishnah also is the Tosefta, ca. 300–400 C.E., a compilation of supplements of various kinds to the statements in the Mishnah. That brings us to Midrash-compilations. There were three systematic exegeses of books of Scripture or the written Torah tied to the Mishnah because, in passages, they may cite the Mishnah or the Tosefta verbatim and raise interesting questions about the relationship between the Mishnah or the Tosefta and Scripture. These Midrash-compilations are the *Sifra*, to Leviticus, *Sifré to Numbers*, and another *Sifré*, to Deuteronomy. These books overall form one stage in the unfolding of the Judaism of the dual Torah, oral and written, in which emphasis stressed issues of sanctification of the life of Israel, the people, in the aftermath of the destruction of the Temple of Jerusalem in 70 C.E.

The second set of the writings, 400–600, that culminated in the Bavli stressed the dual issues of sanctification and salvation, presenting a doctrine of Israel's redemption by the Messiah in the model of the sage himself. The amplification of the Mishnah, which led to the first of the two sets of writings, defined the literary expression of the theological program at hand. It begins with the Yerushalmi, addressed to the Mishnah as oral Torah. Alongside, work on the written Torah was carried on through *Genesis Rabbah*, a reading of the Book of Genesis to interpret the history and salvation of Israel today in light of the history and salvation of the patriarchs and matriarchs of old, deemed to form the founders of the family of Israel after the flesh. A second important work, *Leviticus Rabbah*, assigned to about the next half century, ca. 450 C.E., read for the lessons of Israel's salvation the Book of Leviticus, which stresses issues of the sanctification of Israel. So Leviticus was reread for its lessons of how Israel's sanctification in the here and now led to Israel's salvation at the end of time. Finally, the Bavli addressed both Torahs, oral and written, Mishnah and Scripture, within one and the same document — the first of the writings of the Judaism of the dual Torah to do so systematically and extensively. The difference between the Bavli and the earlier writings, therefore, is that while the writers of the Yerushalmi systematically interpreted passages of the Mishnah, and the other documents did the same for books of the written Torah, the authorship of the Bavli did both. Alongside, there were some other treatments of biblical books important in synagogue liturgy, particularly the Five Scrolls (e.g., *Lamentations Rabbati*, *Esther Rabbah*, and the like). A remarkable compilation of scriptural lessons pertinent to the special occasions of the synagogue, *Pesiqta de Rab Kahana*, reached closure at the same time (the fifth or sixth century) as well.

The first of the two sets of writings, from the Mishnah to the Yerushalmi, exhibits no sign of interest in or response to the advent of Christianity. The second, from the Yerushalmi forward, appears to respond to and counter the challenge of Christianity. The point of difference, of course, is that from the beginning of the legalization of Christianity in the early fourth century to the establishment of Christianity at the end of that same century Jews in the Land of Israel found themselves facing a challenge that, prior to Constantine, they had found no compelling reason to consider. The specific crisis came when the Christians pointed to the success of the church in the politics of the Roman state as evidence that Jesus Christ was king of the world, and that his claim to be Messiah and King of Israel had now found vindication. The Judaic documents that reached closure in the century after these events attended to questions of salvation—for example, doctrine of history and of the Messiah, authority of the sages' reading of Scripture over against the Christians' interpretation, and the like—that had earlier not enjoyed extensive consideration. Now to some definitions of the words used in this book.

AGGADAH — *See* Halakhah and Aggadah.

ALLEGORY—Telling a story in regard to one matter, while intending a message concerning another matter; reading one thing into another.

CANON—The official or authoritative books of a religious system; the holy books selected from a broad number of possibilities and given the status of revealed truth.

DEAD SEA SCROLLS—Writings found near the Dead Sea from 1947 onward, now assigned to Essene Judaism and often called "the Essene library of Qumran" for the nearby village of Khirbet Qumran. These cover both texts of the Hebrew Bible and apocryphal books and also documents of the community itself, governing its life and stating its theology.

DUAL TORAH—The Judaism of the dual Torah maintains that at Sinai God revealed the Torah, or revelation, to Moses, for formulation and transmission in two media, writing and memory. The *written Torah* corresponds to the Hebrew Bible or Old Testament. The *oral Torah* was handed down from prophets to sages until it reached the authorities named in the *Mishnah*. Because those authorities are set in a direct line of transmission of revelation from Sinai, their teachings—the Mishnah and related writings—fall into the category of the oral Torah.

HALAKHAH AND AGGADAH — *Halakhah*, a word that means "law," refers to how things are done. The word *"aggadah,"* "lore," comes from the root verb meaning "to tell, to report, to narrate"; accordingly, *aggadah* commonly means "narrative or story." It bears the secondary meaning of "fable."

HEBREW BIBLE—The part of Holy Scripture called by Christianity "the Old Testament" and by Judaism "Tanakh."

INTERTEXTUALITY—The theory that diverse texts are to be read in light of one another.

MIDRASH — *Midrash* corresponds to the English word "exegesis" and carries the same generic sense. So far as the writers of the Yerushalmi or the Bavli read and interpreted the Mishnah, they engaged in a process of midrash, and so too for Scripture. But the word "midrash" bears a more limited meaning, namely, "interpretation of the Hebrew Scriptures for the purpose of discovering a pertinent rule (in the Mishnah) or theological truth (in Scripture)."

MIDRASH HALAKHAH AND MIDRASH AGGADAH — *Midrash halakhah* means "to derive a rule or a law from a verse of Scripture." One important exercise is to show the relationship of a rule of the Mishnah to a statement found in Scripture, thus proving that the oral Torah restates principles sustained by the (now more authoritative) written Torah. Another exercise will derive a rule not found in the Mishnah from a verse of Scripture. The previously mentioned works, *Sifra* to Leviticus, *Sifré to Numbers*, and the other *Sifré*, to Deuteronomy, all fall into this category. *Midrash aggadah* means "interpretation of a biblical story." Important parts of *Genesis Rabbah* and *Leviticus Rabbah* contain midrash aggadah — amplifications of scriptural stories. The relationship of the Bavli as a document to these two genres of writing is simple. The Bavli's and Yerushalmi's writers included sizable passages of both categories of writing: midrash halakhah and midrash aggadah. But while the Yerushalmi's writers produced a major treatment of the Mishnah and only episodic statements focused upon Scripture, the Bavli's writers, as is clear, built considerable systematic statements out of both types of writing, as it worked its way toward a massive and encyclopedic restatement of both components of the Torah, written and oral.

MISHNAH — A corpus of laws, organized by topics, in sixty-two tractates, divided into six principal divisions, on agriculture; appointed times; women or family; damages and civil law and government; holy things concerning the everyday conduct of the Temple and maintenance of its buildings; and purities, on the process of cultic contamination (such as is specified in Leviticus) and the removal of that uncleanness. The document was produced in ca. 200 C.E. and the relevant divisions, in particular the second, third, and fourth, were quickly adopted, as the basis for the government of the Jews of the Land of Israel (Palestine) by their ethnarch, Judah the Patriarch, and of the Jews of Babylonia by their ethnarch, the Exilarch or ruler of the Jews of the exile. Ongoing amplification and commentary to the Mishnah produced two Talmuds — one in the Land of Israel, the other in Babylonia — each serving that same basic law code as an extended compilation of rulings and analytical discourse.

PARABLE — Figurative speech which may contain an element of allegory or metaphor, or elements of both; bearing a "deeper" level of meaning than the surface-level meaning.

PARAPHRASE — A translation of a passage from one language to another in which the original is given not word for word but in other language, meant to amplify and explain the original, conveying its sense rather than its exact formulation.

PESHER — An interpretation or explanation of a verse of Scripture, in which a given statement (e.g., of a prophet) is identified with an event or personality in the present time.

RABBAH — Augmented, larger, e.g., *Genesis Rabbah*, the compilation of exegeses of the Book of Genesis which augments and clarifies its meaning.

RABBINIC — From "rabbi," meaning, "my lord," hence, in our own language, simply "mister." "Rabbi" was a title of honor employed in Aramaic and

Hebrew. It was accorded to many of the Judaic sages represented in the Mishnah and the Talmuds and Midrash-compilations and came to apply to the Judaism defined by those authorities and set forth in those writings, hence, "rabbinic Judaism." In this book, that Judaism is called "the Judaism of the dual Torah" (*see* Dual Torah).

SAGES — Holy men–lawyers–philosophers–theologians who formed the authority of the Judaism of the dual Torah and composed its writings and staffed its institutions.

SIFRA—The rabbinic commentary to the Book of Leviticus.

SIFRÉ—The rabbinic commentary to the Book of Numbers and to the Book of Deuteronomy.

TALMUD — As a generic term, "Talmud" refers to a systematic commentary to the Mishnah produced between ca. 200 and 600. There are two Talmuds: one written in the Land of Israel and redacted at ca. 400 C.E. called "the Talmud of the Land of Israel or the Talmud of Jerusalem," and in Hebrew "the Yerushalmi"; the other redacted at ca. 600 C.E. called "the Talmud of Babylonia," or in Hebrew "the Bavli."

TANAKH—The Hebrew word for the Hebrew Bible or Old Testament, made up of the letters *T*, *N*, and *K*, which stand, respectively, for *Torah* or Pentateuch (the Five Books of Moses), *Nebiim* or Prophets, and *Ketubim* or Writings.

TANNAITIC—Pertaining to the teachings or authority of a Tanna, an authority of the first and second centuries C.E. who contributed to the formation of the Mishnah and related writings; "Tanna" means "one who repeats," as in the oral formulation and transmission of a memorized tradition.

TARGUM—Translation of the Hebrew Scriptures into Aramaic; plural: Targumim.

TAXON—A classification, a category; plural: taxa.

TOSEFTA—The rabbinic compilation of supplementary rules, augmenting the Mishnah.

For Further Reading

Two sizable bibliographies serve readers as a base for further study: (1) Lee Haas, "Bibliography on Midrash," in *The Study of Ancient Judaism*, ed. Jacob Neusner (New York: Ktav, 1981), 1:93–106. She provides an extensive account of Midrash-editions as well as studies of and commentaries upon them. (2) Joseph M. Davis, "Bibliography on the Story in Ancient Judaism," in my *New Perspectives on Ancient Judaism*, Studies in Judaism (Lanham, Md.: Univ. Press of America, 1987) 3:185–218. Nearly all of Davis's five hundred bibliography entries are pertinent to the meaning and uses of Midrash in the narrative framework.

See also Gary G. Porton, "Defining Midrash," in my *Study of Ancient Judaism*, 1:55–94; idem, *Understanding Rabbinic Midrash: Texts and Commentary* (Hoboken, N.J.: Ktav, 1985) — a first-rate anthology with an excellent introduction.

These bibliographical studies and introductions provide ample accounts of the available translations of Midrash-compilations as well as introductions to that mode of biblical exegesis.

This book comes at the end of a somewhat protracted set of researches of mine and draws upon translations and analytical ideas that I have worked out in my various publications.

WORKS BY JACOB NEUSNER

Issues of Literary Criticism
Canon and Connection: Intertextuality in Judaism, Studies in Judaism (Lanham, Md.: Univ. Press of America, 1986). This book addresses the theory that all canonical documents of the Judaism of the dual Torah, including Midrash-compilations, may be read in light of all others, without paying atten-

111

tion to the context defined by the particular documents' respective interests and theological concerns. I argue with contemporary representations of the Torah-literature as seamless and bounded only at the outer edges by the canon as a whole. I test that view against the documents themselves and find it difficult to adduce literary evidence in favor of this theological proposition.

Midrash and Literature: The Primacy of Documentary Discourse, Studies in Judaism (Lanham, Md.: Univ. Press of America, 1987). This book contends with the position of James Kugel that the principal and generative setting for Midrash is the discrete biblical verse and argues to the contrary that a given Midrash-exegesis is to be interpreted to begin with in the context of the Midrash-document that presents the Midrash-exegesis. This work goes over the same problem as my volume on *Intertextuality*, but in dialogue with Kugel's definition of Midrash.

History and Context of Midrash in Rabbinic Judaism

Midrash in Context: Exegesis in Formative Judaism, vol. 1 of *The Foundations of Judaism* (Philadelphia: Fortress Press, 1983). This and the next work form a constructive program, one on history, the other on literature. In *Midrash in Context* I present a theory on where, when, and why the sages or rabbis who defined the Judaism of the dual Torah undertook the labor of making Midrash-compilations and Midrash-exegeses. That theory is expanded in *Self-Fulfilling Prophecy: Exile and Return in the History of Judaism* (Boston: Beacon Press, 1987) in the larger context of the Judaic response to the triumph of Christianity after Constantine.

The Workings of Midrash: Major Trends in Rabbinic Bible Interpretation (San Francisco: Harper & Row, 1987). This book continues the constructive exercise of saying what Midrash is, rather than what it is not, and I here examine the three principal trends of rabbinic Bible interpretation, and spell out, with ample illustrations, the workings of each. These are, specifically, exegeses that yield propositions; propositions that yield exegeses; and narrative representations of biblical themes and topics. In this way I have tried to organize all of the diverse data of Midrash into an intelligible pattern. *The Workings of Midrash* does not duplicate *What Is Midrash?*

Monographs

1. *Aphrahat and Judaism: The Christian Jewish Argument in Fourth Century Iran.* Leiden: Brill, 1971. Compares Judaic and Christian exegesis in their polemical context.

2. *Development of Legend: Studies on the Traditions Concerning Yohanan ben Zakkai.* Leiden: Brill, 1970. Studies the formation of the traditions on Yohanan, including the Midrash-traditions assigned to him.

3. *A History of the Mishnaic Law of Purities.* VII. *Negaim.* Leiden: Brill, 1975. Shows the traits of an early rabbinic compilation of exegeses.

4. *The Integrity of Leviticus Rabbah: The Problem of the Autonomy of a Rabbinic Document.* Brown Judaic Studies. Chico, Calif.: Scholars Press, 1985.

5. *Comparative Midrash: The Plan and Program of Genesis Rabbah and Leviticus Rabbah.* Brown Judaic Studies. Atlanta: Scholars Press, 1986.

FOR FURTHER READING

6. *The Foundations of Judaism. Method, Teleology, Doctrine:* Vols. I: *Midrash in Context: Exegesis in Formative Judaism;* II: *Messiah in Context: Israel's History and Destiny in Formative Judaism;* III: *Torah: From Scroll to Symbol in Formative Judaism.* Philadelphia: Fortress Press, 1983–85. [*The Foundations of Judaism.* Philadelphia: Fortress Press, 1987. Abridged edition of the trilogy.]

7. *The Oral Torah: The Sacred Books of Judaism. An Introduction.* San Francisco: Harper & Row, 1985.

8. *Scriptures from the Oral Torah: Sanctification and Salvation in the Sacred Books of Judaism.* San Francisco: Harper & Row, 1987.

9. *The Workings of Midrash: Major Trends in Rabbinic Bible Interpretation.* San Francisco: Harper & Row, 1987.

10. *From Tradition to Imitation. The Plan and Program of Pesiqta Rabbati and Pesiqta de Rab Kahana.* Atlanta: Scholars Press, 1987.

Translations

1. *The Talmud of the Land of Israel: A Preliminary Translation and Explanation.* Vols. IX–XII, XIV–XV, XVII–XXXV. Chicago: Univ. of Chicago Press, 1982–89. Translates all of the Midrash-exegeses in the Talmud of the Land of Israel.

2. *The Talmud of Babylonia: An American Translation.* Brown Judaic Studies. Chico, Calif.: Scholars Press, 1984–85. Translates the Midrash-exegeses for these listed tractates: Vols. I: *Berakhot;* VI: *Sukkah;* XXIII.A: *Sanhedrin 1–3;* XXIII.B: *Sanhedrin 4–8;* XXIII.C.: *Sanhedrin 9–11;* XXXII: *Arakhin.*

3. *Judaism and Scripture: The Evidence of Leviticus Rabbah.* Chicago: Univ. of Chicago Press, 1986. Fresh translation of M. Margulies's text and systematic analysis of problems of composition and redaction.

4. *Genesis Rabbah: The Judaic Commentary on Genesis* (A New American Translation). Vols. I: *Parashiyyot 1–33. Genesis 1:1–8:14;* II: *Parashiyyot 34–67. Genesis 8:15–28:9;* III: *Parashiyyot 68–100. Genesis 28:10–50:26.* Brown Judaic Studies. Atlanta: Scholars Press, 1985.

5. *Sifra: The Judaic Commentary on Leviticus* (A New Translation). *The Leper. Leviticus 13:1–14:57.* Brown Judaic Studies. Chico, Calif.: Scholars Press, 1985. Based on the translation of *Sifra Parashiyyot Negaim* and *Mesora* in *A History of the Mishnaic Law of Purities.* VI: *Negaim. Sifra* (with a section by Roger Brooks).

6. *Sifré to Numbers* (An American Translation). Vols. I: *1–58;* II: *59–115;* III: *116–61,* trans. William Scott Green. Brown Judaic Studies. Atlanta: Scholars Press, 1986.

7. *The Fathers According to Rabbi Nathan (An Analytical Translation and Explanation).* Brown Judaic Studies. Atlanta: Scholars Press, 1987.

8. *Pesiqta de Rab Kahana* (An Analytical Translation and Explanation). Vols. I: *1–14;* II: *23–28 (with an Introduction to Pesiqta de Rab Kahana).* Brown Judaic Studies. Atlanta: Scholars Press, 1987.

9. *Sifre to Deuteronomy.* Vols. I–II. Brown Judaic Studies. Atlanta: Scholars Press, 1987.

10. *Sifra. An American Translation.* Brown Judaic Studies. Atlanta: Scholars Press, 1988.

Edited Anthologies

1. *Goodenough's Jewish Symbols: An Abridged Edition*. Princeton: Princeton Univ. Press, 1986. On the expression of Midrash-exegesis in art.

2. *Torah from Our Sages: Pirke Avot* (A New American Translation and Explanation). Chappaqua, N.Y.: Rossel, 1983, 1986.

3. *Our Sages, God, and Israel: An Anthology of the Yerushalmi*. Chappaqua, N.Y.: Rossel, 1984.

4. *Genesis and Judaism: The Perspective of Genesis Rabbah. An Analytical Anthology*. Brown Judaic Studies. Atlanta: Scholars Press, 1986.

5. *Christian Faith and the Bible of Judaism*. Grand Rapids: Wm. B. Eerdmans, 1987.

6. *Reading Scriptures: An Introduction to Rabbinic Midrash. With Special Reference to Genesis Rabbah*. Dallas: Rossel, 1987.

7. *From Testament to Torah: An Introduction to Judaism in Its Formative Age*. Englewood Cliffs, N.J.: Prentice-Hall, 1987.